THE PORTRAIT

of

ZÉLIDE

GEOFFREY SCOTT

THE PORTRAIT

of

ZÉLIDE

INTRODUCTION BY SHIRLEY HAZZARD

AFTERWORD BY RICHARD DUNN

HELEN MARX

A TURTLE POINT IMPRINT

NEW YORK

FIRST PUBLISHED IN GREAT BRITAIN
BY CONSTABLE & CO.

COPYRIGHT © 1997 TURTLE POINT PRESS
INTRODUCTION © 1997 COPYRIGHT SHIRLEY HAZZARD
AFTERWORD © 1997 COPYRIGHT RICHARD DUNN

ISBN: 1-885983-19-0
LIBRARY OF CONGRESS CATALOG CARD NUMBER: 96-060613

DESIGN AND COMPOSITION BY
WILSTED & TAYLOR PUBLISHING SERVICES

PRINTED IN THE U.S.A.

TO *Sybil*

INTRODUCTION

Her early life evokes its eighteenth-century setting:
a flat, fixed, ordered scene of Dutch manors and
villages; of fields extending, almost level, to the cold
sea. Overhead, a huge sky of changing light and
measureless possibility. Her circumstances are cul-
tivated, wealthy, well born; her immediate family
affectionate, exemplary, conventional, confining.
As she grows—as she enters "Society" and her twenties—singularities of temperament assert themselves. Unaffected, merry, flippant, confident, she
possesses a measure of genius. To an exceptional degree, she is both formidable and enchanting, playful
and obdurate. And "I must tell you, too, that Zélide
herself is handsome," so James Boswell writes to her,
using the name she has whimsically adopted; James
Boswell, a captivated admirer and equivocal suitor.

We hear nothing of female friendships. Her
mother is dear to her, and indulgent. Her sister is resentful, and a bore.

Zélide's wit and beauty, her prodigious intelligence are not without arrogance. For most of her life,
however, pride will be countered by a disarming
honesty of self-appraisal. Her Gallic rationality is
similarly moderated by cordiality. Among her finest

attributes is simplicity of conduct: springing from people disposed to take themselves seriously, she has little taste for self-solemnity. Free of national pride, she would, in later years, tell her dearest correspondent: "You and I, in the days of our friendship, were of no country." With all the gaiety and ardour, some sweetness is lacking. It is, again, Boswell who reproaches her for according her goodwill indiscriminately: "Every one is at his ease with you. It is terrible." He reminds her that a man—and even such an ambivalent suitor as himself—likes to enjoy primacy. For the same offence, the autocratic husband of Browning's "Last Duchess" had his wife put to death:

> She had a heart—how shall I say?—too soon
>   made glad . . .
> She liked whate'er she looked on, and her looks
>   went everywhere . . .
> She smiled, no doubt, whene'er I passed her;
>   but who passed without
> Much the same smile?

Yes, for love some particular tenderness is necessary. And the reader, hoping—naturally enough—for love, will have to follow Zélide through much curious experience before the unexpected requital.

Her qualities bring her renown, and distinguished correspondents. Having seen her portrait, the King of Prussia advises her to "give up reading Fénelon."

She acknowledges that marriage, children, would be a solution—if commonplace—to her dichotomy of temperament, and to an increasingly motiveless life. Of herself she writes that she is secretly "somewhat sensuous." Projects for wedding her fall through—not always through her own reluctance. In what she acknowledges to be an unattractive episode, she labours, vainly, to bring an unenthusiastic candidate to the altar—principally in order to draw closer to the man most worthy, and most appreciative, of her youthful powers. Constant d'Hermenches, the secret epistolary confidant whom she rarely saw, was himself married. In their letters, at least, he and Zélide are intimates; in letters, they are lovers. During those years, he said, her radiance would have warmed the heart of a Laplander.

At thirty, she marries. In 1773, Isabella van Serooskerken van Tuyll becomes Madame de Charrière, choosing from among more notable suitors a prosaic, undemonstrative—but not unfeeling—pedant, the former tutor of her brothers. There is nothing inevitable in that wilful decision, seemingly taken at random. There have been many encounters in her life, and many advantages; there have been travels, and much exposure to favourable chance; there has been such an unusual degree of independence that the choice must seem irrational. She cannot easily be claimed as a victim—of her sex, her era, her society. By now, she might be charged with a few victims of her own. She removes herself to her husband's modest château near Lausanne (where, although within easy distance of Ferney, she chooses not to meet Voltaire). The sky of possibilities, the open sea, the world of travel and discourse are now remote. Mountains and winter fogs enclose her; the lake is seldom stirred. The future is contracting.

Years pass. Merriment has no occasion. Intellect and rationality turn bleakly inward. She writes animated and interesting novels—whose autobiographical aspects alienate her neighbours and wound the husband who patiently copies out her manuscripts. Her writings are talented and apposite; their purpose is not merely vengeful. Introducing a volume of her fiction that appeared in translation in 1926, Geoffrey Scott points out that her impulse "was to use all this tedium to good effect. . . . Her subject is human nature; she watches it in herself." Writing, publishing, does not relieve her spirits. An obscure local love affair disappoints her, intensifying what has become despair.

Why does she stay? Why not return to the world? Why not separate—or, as she might have done, divorce?

One summer, retreating to the mountains, she is visited by her grieved and excluded husband; who, on return to his gloomy house, writes her a sad, fine letter that must have touched but could not melt her heart—that heart, one thinks, by now more deeply frozen than any Laplander's. Years earlier, Boswell, dazzled as he was, had told her: "I fear the heart of Zélide is not to be found." Not, certainly, by usual avenues.

Commentators have cautioned us not to insist unduly on the legendary analogy of her suspended life: the sequestered princess languishing for want of rightful awakening. All the same, the fable irresistibly comes to mind—in her case, enigmatically self-imposed. Nothing in all Zélide's unpredictable existence is more unlikely than the irruption of the brilliant boy, nearly thirty years her junior, who—first encountered during a rare visit to Paris—breaks through brambles and cold Swiss walls to bring her back to life: to bring her liveliness, love, and that intimacy of spirit, intellect, wit, and affection in which, perhaps, she had always believed but never trusted.

Benjamin Constant loved her; and paid tribute to her to the end of his life. The ironic surname of this mercurial prodigy was, ultimately, valid in relation to her.

> We suited each other perfectly. But it was not long before we found ourselves in a relation of more real and essential intimacy. Madame de Charrière's outlook on life was so original and lively, her contempt for conventional prejudices so profound, her intellect so forceful, her superiority to average nature so

vigorous and assured, that for me, a boy of twenty, as eccentric and scornful as herself, her company was a joy such as I had never yet known. I gave myself up to it rapturously.

Not since the correspondence with Hermenches—who, into the bargain, is Benjamin's uncle—has Zélide responded full-heartedly to another human soul. She has somehow maintained, through arid years, her best readiness of self and sensibility, her laughter, and the luminous generosity of her mind. One feels the release of it, her emancipation. She and Benjamin are happy, not only in their boundless affinity but, as lovers are, in one another's unstinted presence. Monsieur de Charrière himself enjoys Benjamin's company—partly, no doubt, because of the enlivening change wrought in his hitherto martyred wife; partly because of the reassuring discrepancy of age; and in part, perhaps, because Benjamin is fascinating, funny, and endearing.

Benjamin sits by her fire, by her desk, by her bed. We do not know how to define that reference to a "more real and essential intimacy."

Geoffrey Scott tells us that

The hours went their round. And sometimes when the fire was steady or a single candle burned between them, he would watch the dark silhouette of her profile on the wall, and note the elusive beauty that even her shadow possessed.

Thus, for eight years, Benjamin comes and goes. Her house, for him, represents serenity, stimulus, pleasure, and rigorous thought. They correspond, and his letters become love letters. Despite the convolutions of a libertine existence and divided personality, he sometimes dreams, preposterously, of eloping with her. Much about Benjamin Constant is preposterous—not excepting the preternatural comprehension in which his genius is rooted; and which, exercised on his own psychology and extraordinary life will, in his writings, secure his posterity.

Zélide not only fears the fated rupture, but anxiously precipitates it: as ever, she is over-endowed with rational foresight and with a faculty for self-injury. Their parting, when it comes at last, is sublime—and perhaps, she feels, not conclusive. When the subsequent dénouement arrives, however, she is astonished and appalled. Benjamin has moved away—but a few miles only: to Coppet, on the Lake of Geneva. Thereafter—and again, this time, for years and famously—he will linger there, in chaotic thrall to Zélide's volcanic neighbour, the brawny and brave Madame de Staël. Detaching himself from Enlightenment, he embraces Romanticism—and embraces, unequivocally, Germaine de Staël. His years with her, unenviably dramatic, will carry him into political and literary adventures, and turbulent *amours*. He will father a child, he will marry, divorce—and re-marry the same wife. He will cut a figure both of folly and courage in the world of action. He will never lose his gift of observation and self-appraisal; and will turn it, uniquely, to literary account.

For Zélide, pride and a haughty resignation consume the remaining years. Her very submission resembles an act of iron will, further dispiriting her husband. ("It is recorded that for fifteen years she never took a walk outside the walls of his garden.") She continues to write—but now these are dry writings that defend logic and reason through the convulsed years that conclude the eighteenth-century. She performs acts of humanity and philanthropy, befriending solitary—and even outcast—young women, who find her admirable but . . . intimidating.

With the passage of years, she corresponds occasionally with Benjamin—who, struggling now in the toils of Madame de Staël, thinks tenderly of Zélide, and of the concord and delight of their shared years. Acknowledging the lack of synthesis in her being and her destiny, she tells him: "My life and my memories have no unity; my plan of life had none."

As that life closes, she is regarded with awe by those few familiars who attend her. At her death, in 1805, she is sixty-five, and has spent more than thirty years by the cold lake—perplexing, aloof; and disclosing only briefly her concealed fires, her great capacity for companionship and love.

It was Francis Steegmuller who drew my attention to *The Portrait of Zélide*—seeing Geoffrey Scott's earlier work, *The Architecture of Humanism*, on my shelves, and referring to "Zélide" as a favourite work of his since youth. During the subsequent years of our marriage, *The Portrait of Zélide*, in different editions, was among books that accumulated in our rooms abroad—in France, in Italy. In every reading life, certain works are talismans, especially those read in early years. Francis had discovered "Zélide" soon after its first publication, when he was in his twenties; and he felt that it had influenced him toward the writing of biography, which would occupy the greater part of his working life.

He loved the book—for relating, with sympathetic intelligence, with integrity and beauty, the story of an engrossing life. He admired the close attention to established evidence and existing scholarship, and the truthful ease with which these were incorporated in the narrative, contributing to its authority and surprise. The period and its *mentalité*, and the culture of the Enlightenment, were already strong interests for him. With this work, Geoffrey Scott undoubtedly stimulated those affinities. Another theme that would develop and recur in Francis Steegmuller's writing is embodied in *The Portrait of Zélide*: that of the intelligent and gifted woman seeking to ripen and express her best powers; yet carrying within her an ideal of love unlikely to be realised.

The Grande Mademoiselle, Isadora Duncan, Louise d'Épinay all became subjects for books by Francis. He considered, and made preparatory studies for, biographies—never completed—of Anna Comnena, the first woman historian; of Marie Mancini; and of Queen Christina. All those interests may owe, initially, something to his feeling for the story of *Zélide*.

When Scott's book appeared, in 1925, the name of Isabella van Tuyll was virtually unknown to the English-reading world. Despite much serious scholarship since then, and recent publication of her writings in France, Britain, and the United States, she is scarcely today a household word. Geoffrey Scott, who died in 1929, at the age of forty-five, was a forerunner, and has occasionally been accorded, by subsequent scholars, a condescension sometimes shown to precursors. Nonetheless, the literary intelligence and sensibility, the command of language with which Scott tells this story are qualities to be praised and envied. No one who reads *The Portrait of Zélide* will forget it. The book is unique, it is humane, it is delightful. It is art.

Shirley Hazzard

THE PORTRAIT OF ZÉLIDE

I

LA TOUR HAS PAINTED MADAME DE CHARRIÈRE: a face too florid for beauty, a portrait of wit and wilfulness where the mind and senses are disconcertingly alert; a temperament impulsive, vital, alarming; an arrowy spirit, quick, amusing, amused.

Houdon has left of her a bust in his fine manner: a distinguished head, a little sceptical and aloof.

Both portraits are convincing; both were applauded as faithful likenesses by this lady and her admirers.

The interest to us of her life, its unadmitted but evident tragedy to her, is there in these two interpretations, both real, of a character so avid of living, so sceptical of life, which could find no harmony within itself nor acquiesce in the discord.

Madame de Charrière was not of marble, emphatically, nor even of the hardness of Houdon's clay. But the coldness of Houdon's bust—its touch of aloofness—corresponds to an intellectual ideal, more masculine than feminine, which she set before herself. It embodies a certain harsh clear cult of the reason which at every crisis falsified her life. She was not more reasonable, in the last resort, than the rest

I

of humanity. She paid in full and stoically, the penalty of supposing herself to be so.

La Tour was nearer the truth: the painted shadow is less conventional than the carven image, and colour, with its changing lights, a little nearer to the stuff of which we are made.

But even in La Tour's portrait, which misses her scepticism, it is not easy to see how the subject of it could well achieve happiness, or make others happy. Madame de Charrière, who entered on life with so confident a will to these two human ends, knew as she lay dying in that desolate Swiss manor, her chosen exile, that she had failed, immensely and poignantly, of both.

Isabella van Serooskerken van Tuyll—to give Madame de Charrière her Dutch name—was born at the château of Zuylen in 1740 of one of the oldest families in Holland. To give her a Dutch name: that was the first freak of malice which Providence played on this surprising woman. Every physical and moral law, she used to say, must have been suspended in the circumstances of so paradoxical a nativity. A Dutch woman and a Tuyll—she felt herself in every fibre of mind and nature a stranger to that phlegmatic world. The van Tuylls were famous even among the old-fashioned nobility of Holland for a stolid virtue, a conventional probity, a profound pride of birth. By what trick of heredity had "Belle de Zuylen" sprung from that grave, imposing stock—she, with her mocking spirit, so eager, so unquiet?

The background of her life was the great moated house at Zuylen, from whose walls innumerable van Tuylls looked down in stiff disapproval of their too lively descendant; where *mynvrow* sat upright at her needlework and *mynheer* with placid rectitude sat thinking about the dykes. Outside, a Cuyp landscape with eternal cattle motionlessly browsing—were they too thinking of the public good?—and somewhere a solitary horseman slowly, slowly ambling—perhaps a Tuyll, mindful of his *"droit de chasse."* Truly a land where it was always afternoon, nay Sunday afternoon: a land where nothing ever happened—where nothing ever ought to happen—to ruffle the dead surface of that Tuyll serenity, born of many quarterings and an unblemished life. The Romans of the great days of Rome were not more virtuous, she said. But those great days of Rome were not very gay either, and Zuylen was more provincial than the Seven Hills.

In winter the scene changed to Utrecht, to that other grave house, damp and gentlemanly and bordered by the still canal. On one side the empty street, on the other the severe garden; a place of austere dignity, sombre in winter and silent. But sometimes, within, candles lit up the quiet stateliness of the shadowy rooms, and faultless dowagers would assemble for polite and disapproving talk. *Andante* was signed upon their conversation: no wide ideas, no quick emotion ever jarred that scrupulous society. Across this decent picture of still-life Belle de Zuylen moved, a single unquenched flame of lonely animation, *"Ici l'on est vif tout seul."*

The van Tuylls were sincere folk; it was one of their almost too numerous virtues. In Belle this traditional sincerity took the form of a disconcerting frankness. Impatient of restraint, conscious in herself of a fundamental goodwill, she placed no bridle on her feverish spirit, her Voltairean wit, her subversive criticism of accepted values. She wished to be "a citizen of the country of all the world"—a natural ideal to one whose sympathy and curiosity were, from the first, amazingly wide. She brought a French quickness, an English *sans-gêne*, and (on her own confession) some ardent touches of the South, into a slow and solemn and passionless Dutch world. It was as though a firework were to go off—to keep going off—at a nice, orderly funeral.

Very orderly; very sedate and genteel. Nevertheless in Belle's parents—and she was the first to admit it—there was nothing unduly puritanical or harsh. "My father," she wrote, "is a man accustomed to the paintings of a smiling landscape: he averts his eyes from the horrors of a tempest or St. Laurence's gridiron or the Last Judgment. The family dictionary is modelled on his thought. No exclamations, no lively expressions, nothing shocking." A good man, courteous and unaffected; a governor of the Province, conscientiously discharging his duty, and happy in works of building or administration, Monsieur de Tuyll's only fault was to set a standard of virtue so high that one felt, in his presence, at a kind of moral disadvantage. "I never feel satisfied with myself in regard to him," is Belle's reflection; for it was characteristic of her that she wanted the prize for goodness as well as the forbidden fruit. For the rest, he hated to interfere, and preferred not to notice whatever he might have to disapprove. He opposed a *fin de non recevoir* to her "lively expressions," and could he have seen into the very unconventional process of his daughter's heart, or caught a glimpse of certain pages of her correspondence, no doubt he would have averted his eyes as from the gridiron of Saint Laurence.

The mother, thanks to her less noble origin, was more amenable. She had caught the Tuyll note: lively expressions had long since ceased to cross her kindly lips; but she was "known to joke" and capitulated readily enough to an attack upon her sense of humour. And when disaster came, and those illicit letters did fall into her possession, she got over it. Belle was at pains to persuade her that, with it all, she was as good, nay better than another. *"Et je voulais faire avouer à ma mère que telle que j'étais je valais encore mieux qu'une autre."* The prize for goodness once more.

Tuyll to the bone, on the contrary, was the younger daughter, Jeanne-Marie. She figures but seldom in her sister's letters; we discern her, clearly enough, tight, prim, conventional: a good girl, and likely to remain so. Plainly a prude, and favoured with a prettiness which failed to please, Jeanne distilled an atmosphere of disapproval not untainted with jealousy. She was, Belle frankly states, the kind of sister one would love better were she in America: in home life she showed a sulky temper and a taste for scenes of sentimental reconciliation conducted with unbearable solemnity. She married in due course a serious Dutchman who nevertheless consented to become the intermediary of that clandestine correspondence with Constant d'Hermenches in which Belle revealed herself so winningly—free, kindly, gay, spontaneous, Jeanne's opposite at every point.

There were four brothers; the eldest was drowned while bathing, at eighteen; of the second she writes, "William is always out hunting, or else ill from having hunted too much: his temper is uncertain, his manner often hard and uncivil." She reads Plutarch with Vincent: "I try to separate in his mind the conceptions of *book* and *pain*." ("Why is it," she once asked, "that the young should only know two categories of books—those they are forced to read, and those they read in secret?") Vincent is slow, prudent, and systematic: in short, very Tuyll. He becomes a soldier, and Belle proposes to console herself for his loss by learning to play upon the lute. But Dietrich, three years older than Vincent, is her favourite. A simple-minded sailor, he returns from his long voyages and cannot leave his sister's side; he sits on her bed at all hours listening to conversations "unlike anything in the world" and confiding his naïve love affairs. Later on, it is to Dietrich that some of her most charming letters are addressed. He died, to her great sorrow, of consumption, in 1773.

If the problem of life had to be settled once for all on a fixed pattern, if no ideas should be revised and few be suffered to exist, this life at Zuylen, so harmless, so safely decent, and, all in all, so equably harmonious, might serve as well as any for the chosen type. But, for Madame de Charrière, ideas were the breath of existence, and life presented itself to her not as a tradition but as a great experiment. This proposition—that the world should be ruled by ideas and not by customs, was in itself the newest of ideas. Belle de Zuylen, alone in the world of Tuylls, had caught the breath of the new spirit which thirty years later was to make the Revolution. If she seemed eccentric to her countrymen, it was because she appealed at every point from usage to reason: her true eighteenth-century mind could not doubt for a moment that logic was the basis of human happiness. That man is an irrational animal, for whom logic lays a snare; that custom, like the heart, has its own reasons; that folly, as a human attribute, is entitled, if not to veneration, at least to a certain tenderness, she could not conceive. Yet, where her parents were concerned, an instinctive kindliness and a touch, perhaps, of Tuyll pride in their heroic sense of caste impelled her to obedience. "I could not change their ideas, and they will never change their conduct so long as their principles remain unchanged. Their intentions are pure, and they are firm, as they ought to be, in doing what to them seems right. If there is any excess on their side, I ought not, on mine, to submit myself the less to their will. I could not pardon myself if I caused them pain." That is, in plain English, she followed her own fancy, and tried to prevent them from finding it out.

From the outer world she had less regard, and her demeanour was not calculated to disarm it. The downcast eyes and modest blushes, which were looked for by Dutch dowagers in one of her age, were not in Belle de Zuylen's repertoire. "*Une demoiselle, cela, une demoiselle!*" exclaimed Madame d'Aincourt, seeing her sail into their midst with her whimsical *sans-gêne* and merry superiority. There were rumours, perhaps, of that clandestine correspondence, there was the certainty that she had actually published a very lively satire, "Le Noble," in mockery of their respect for quarterings, there was *une belle gorge, dont elle se pare trop*, a little too much in evidence, "*Une demoiselle . . . cela!*"

It is clear that to Belle de Zuylen the breath of

8

public censure was not altogether displeasing. Or rather, she met disapproval as a natural consequence of her merits. The stupidity of most people being a plain *datum* of experience, she was too logical to desire their praise in any matter of the reason. And since reason was for her the key to everything, she accepted her isolation as a necessary fact. With it all, people were happier with her than away from her; she had in her a fire of vitality to which her coldest critics loved to hold their hands. As Hermenches said, she could warm the heart of a Laplander.

Her gaiety, which illumined the shadowy world she moved in, was nevertheless the mask to a profound melancholy. She was one of those whose inmost consciousness is born sceptical, and she was disillusioned even before life had destroyed the illusions she artificially created. Those around her who envied and caught the glow of her seeming happiness were in less need of it than herself; their very dullness was a kindly anaesthetic: they asked no ultimate questions and hungered for no ultimate satisfactions. "No one guesses," she writes, "that I am a prey to the darkest gloom: I can find health, nay, life itself, only by means of a ceaseless occupation of the mind."

The occupation was ceaseless indeed; at thirteen she must be up at six to study mathematics; later, she is "determined to master Newton"; she "hates half learnings" and wishes "to know all that can be known in our time of physics"—a programme which must not exclude a decent proficiency on the harpsichord; she is deep in all the properties of conic sections. The vital fire burnt brightly on this stubborn fuel: "I find an hour or two of mathematics gives me a freer mind and a light heart; I eat and sleep better when I have grasped an evident and indisputable truth." Mathematics consoled her for the obscurity of religion: that door had been closed to her once for all by the minister who, in preparing her for confirmation, thought her scruples unworthy of discussion. For in Belle's mind a proposition must be as clear as Euclid or it was nothing.

Yet all this was not fuel enough. Plutarch, first and foremost, then Pascal, Madame de Sevigné, St. Evremond, Hamilton, and Voltaire:—these rivalled even the indisputable truth of conic sections; and she never travelled "without Racine and Molière in my box and Fontaine in my memory." From the earliest years French was the language of her thought. In French she wrote poetry, or what passed for such, and prose of a high order, lucid, witty, and sane. "You write better than anyone known to me, not excepting Voltaire," said Hermenches, a friendly critic it is true; "the authentic tongue of Versailles" is the verdict of Sainte-Beuve.

One autumn evening she beguiled the tedium of her Dutch life by composing a slight essay on her own character. She saw herself very accurately. And the last words of this paper, written at the outset of her life, might truly, when her story was played out, have been written on her grave.

She called it *"The Portrait of Mlle. de Z., under the name of Zélide."*

"Compassionate in temper and liberal by inclination, Zélide is patient only on principle; when she is indulgent and easy be grateful to her, for it costs her an effort. When she prolongs her civility with people she holds in small esteem, redouble your admiration: she is in torture. Vain at first by nature, her vanity has become boundless; knowledge and scorn of mankind soon perfected that quality. Yet this vanity is excessive even to her own taste. She already thinks that fame is worth nothing at the cost of happiness, and yet she would make many an effort for fame. . . .

"Would you like to know if Zélide is beautiful, or pretty, or merely passable? I cannot tell; it all depends on whether one loves her, or on whether she wishes to make herself beloved. She has a beautiful neck, and displays it at some sacrifice of modesty. Her hands are not white; she knows that also, and makes a jest of it; but she would rather not have this occasion for jest.

"Excessively emotional, and not less fastidious, she cannot be happy either with or without love. Perceiving herself too sensitive to be happy, she has almost ceased to aspire to happiness and has devoted herself to goodness; she thus escapes repentance and seeks only for diversion.

"Can you not guess her secret? Zélide is somewhat sensuous. Emotions too vivid and too intense for her organism, an exaggerated activity without any satisfying object, these are the source of all her misfortunes. With less sensibility Zélide would have had the mind of a great man; with less intelligence she would have been only a weak woman."

Her tongue was French, and her intelligence; not so her nature. She was averse from all those conventions of gallantry which are founded on pretence. "No doubt a French platitude becomes a hundred times flatter in a Dutch mouth, but, believe me, without the French, a woman with no desire to be loved would not talk so much of the passion of a man who, in fact, does not love her; it would not occur to us to be witty for half an hour on an equivocation; and those light themes, without head, tail, or sense, would never have entered our thick heads." She preferred the English form of sociability, where men who have nothing to say, say nothing. Her own brilliance was always employed to light up a firm sobriety of thought: pose and paradox, mere wit, mere romanticism, she detested in literature as in talk. Frankness was "her favourite virtue"; her passion was for reality of intercourse.

To Mademoiselle de Tuyll's engaging quality of frankness we owe our intimate knowledge of this

lady's chief occupation during the long years at Zuylen and Utrecht. This occupation was not the true
prose of Versailles; it was not Newton, not the harpsichord, nor "all that can be known in our time of
physics"; it was, briefly—getting married.

The theme is one for an epic poet rather than an
essayist, the canvas is so crowded, the action so varied and prolonged, the energy displayed so heroic.
Penelope had not more trouble with her Homeric
suitors, and Mademoiselle de Tuyll was far from
being a Penelope. Her suitors, too, were very different from Penelope's: they had a way of taking flight.
Yes, the prologue of Belle's marriage is epic, decidedly; but the climax was comedy; and the end,
tragedy.

Some twelve suitors are known to history as candidates (or probable candidates) for the hand of Mademoiselle de Tuyll. No doubt there were others.
Her vicissitudes with regard to these twelve were
confided to a thirteenth who, being married, was not
a suitor. This was Constant d'Hermenches, baron de
Rebecque, a dashing Swiss noble in the service of the
Dutch Republic. It was said of Hermenches that he
wished to be, at one and the same moment, courtier
and man of letters, soldier and farmer, scholar and
dévot. Ambition and vanity were clearly marked on
his dark and rather effeminate features; a love of
pleasure, also, and an extreme assurance in procur-
ing it. His career was military, his talents were his-

trionic, his triumphs principally amorous. He was a friend of Voltaire's, with whom he played Orosmane, and of *ces dames*, for whom he played Don Juan. The advent of this brilliant cavalier at the Hague aroused some misgiving and a lively curiosity. Belle marked him down at once; it happened, she reminds him, "four years ago, at the duke's ball . . . *Monsieur, vous ne dansez pas?*" She was not one to be shy of taking the initiative. "With our first words we quarrelled; with our second we were friends for life."

Well, hardly for life; but for twelve years, at least, these two kept up a correspondence of the most singular intimacy. "You are the man in whom, of all the world, I have the completest and most instinctive confidence," she writes, "for you I have no prudence, no reserve, no prudery: nay, what is more remarkable, no vanity either. I am always ready to tell you of every folly which lowers me in my own esteem. If we lived together I would have no secrets from you." It is natural, therefore, that she should write again, "Monsieur, in God's name burn my letters!" But the letters were a great deal too good to burn. And, later, when, before her marriage, Belle made repeated and desperate appeals for the return of the dossier, Hermenches turned a deaf ear on her entreaties. Vanity or a fine taste in literature may have been the motive of his refusal; the result in any case is that a hundred and seventy-eight of these intimate documents repose at this date, duly catalogued, in the public library of Geneva. So fortunate are the consequences of the most inexcusable actions!

If Mademoiselle de Tuyll took the first step in this unconventional friendship, it was she, no less, who dictated the terms of it. "I hear it said on all sides, and even by your admirers, that you are the most dangerous of men and that no caution is too great in dealing with you. . . . The friend I want to keep would not have your eagerness nor your ways of expression. I cannot take all you say as the mere language of politeness: I think, Monsieur, that you are or that you feign to be something more than a friend, and I would wish neither to permit a folly nor be the dupe of a deceit. How can you expect me to look upon you as a man whose advice I can trust? . . . You are for me one of those rare and precious possessions which one is mad enough to wish to obtain and to keep at any price, though one can put them to no use when acquired. I have too much sought your notice and then your esteem, since in the end we have gained so little that we can neither see each other nor write openly."

The situation was characteristic. Belle had capitulated from the start, frankly and without a trace of conventional *amour propre*: "*j'étais éprise de l'empire que vous exerciez sur moi.*" Hermenches, on the other hand, who might seem to have made in her one of the easiest of his conquests, found himself confronted with a will as strong as his own. This masterful woman was always seeking a master: she could never accept one. She could never surrender her reason, and her cold sense of fact perpetually nipped the bud of romance. No one, in that age of gallantry, ever had less use for the comedies of flirtation or wasted less time with the business of coqueterie. She states things exactly as they are: neither more nor less. "It would be easy for me to use all the commonplaces of modesty, to tell you that in seeing me more often you would cease to love me. That would not be true. On the contrary, I think that, whatever small degree of feeling you may have for me at present, you would love me much more in the future. Allow me, Hermenches, the pride of believing that no woman will ever take in your heart precisely the place that I might hold in it. But as for love—all, I mean, that is necessary to enable you to be with me without agitation—you will feel that perhaps, any day, for some more beautiful woman. You will see a thousand whose charms, coupled with a sufficiency of sense, will restore you to all the peace of mind you may desire in regard to me. Since we have known each other, I have never failed to keep your esteem and your predilection; but how many times has your heart been otherwise occupied? . . . It is absolutely necessary that we should write less often, that we should think of each other less. *Ah! Dieu, si jamais, comptant sur vos doigts les femmes qui vous ont trop aimé, je me trouvais entre la Martin et quelque autre de son espèce!"*

Hermenches had to content himself, therefore, with the role of confidant. He writes to her on the tone of worldly wisdom; his letters are a blend of philosophy and gallantry; but, play-actor though he essentially is, his feeling takes by reflection the sincerity of hers. There is a true affection between the pair, and beneath this affection the instinctive war of two consummate egoists. It was, upon the whole, a drawn battle. Belle may seem to impose herself at every point: she chooses her antagonist; she defines the rules of the action; she makes herself the principal figure in the piece. The subject of every letter is herself: it is of her character, her doings, her needs, her aspirations that she writes. But, after all, it is to Hermenches she confides them: his male assurance is satisfied with that; and she, in turn, is dominated by his assurance. "I was in love with the empire you assumed."

They cannot marry: they cannot even meet. Yet he is the audience before whom she enacts her life, and she holds him by his vulnerable point of vanity. That this girl, who might soon be acknowledged in Europe as one of the brilliant women of her time—she who wrote "better than Voltaire"—should declare herself his pupil in the art of living, meant more to this dilettante than all his conquests. Untamed, Belle

flattered his pride more subtly than if she had lowered her worth by a complete surrender. But what
could be the future of such a friendship?

It was as a solution to this problem that Hermenches proposed to marry Mademoiselle de Tuyll
to his best friend, the Marquis de Bellegarde. Hermenches was a constant visitor on his friend's estates;
the separation would thus be less complete. If Hermenches had any *arrière pensée* in making this proposal, Belle is too generous to suspect it. "What you
are doing seems to me a fine, a noble, and a difficult
thing. A person who knew nothing of love might
say—'She cannot be yours; it is therefore no sacrifice
to give her to your friend.' I judge you very differently: I am too much aware that to add, by your own
act, new separations to old, to place a lasting and in-
vincible obstacle in the way of your desires, demands
a courageous and sublime generosity. It is a very different thing to marry the woman you love to your
closest friend, than to acquiesce in her union with
another man."

That "favourite virtue of frankness" in Mademoiselle de Tuyll will be much in evidence in her deal-
ings with the Marquis; but once more she finds herself in a crooked situation. Bellegarde was a Catholic,
the Tuylls were Protestant: pride and conviction
were both involved in the question of faith, and the
obstacle of religion was likely to prove an insuperable one in the eyes of Belle's parents. It was neces-

sary, therefore, to go gently. Monsieur de Bellegarde was neither very ardent nor very adroit; he went too gently; he could hardly be said to go at all. Every stage of his suit had to be planned and carried through by the two conspirators. Belle confesses a scruple—"not for the project itself, which still seems a good one, but for the means to be employed. Sometimes I hate this roundabout path, this sense of plot. I feel that I am guilty towards my father, that I am deceiving him, that you yourself will think I am acting against my honesty and my frankness—the virtue I hold to most and would make the ransom of all my faults. You, Hermenches, must be my casuist; you who know women so well, and how they are judged, must prevent my doing anything unworthy. I would not be despised by the man whose wife I desire to become; above all I would not have him think me false, for that I am not."

The casuist was well chosen, and Mademoiselle de Tuyll, with her qualms sufficiently at rest, set to work with her accustomed energy. The suitable moment at last arrived for approaching the parents, and the inert Marquis entrusted Hermenches with the task of pleading his suit. But characteristically, it was Belle herself who composed the letter of proposal. She informed Hermenches that her father should be addressed in the following terms: "You are, Sir, no less aware than I that the talents which heaven has showered upon your daughter—talents which a distin-

guished education has refined and united with every
virtue—are precious gifts, more desirable in themselves than any alliance however advantageous, yet
capable also of proving an obstacle to such a union.
There are few men in whom those talents do not inspire fear; fewer still who may hope to find favour
with their possessor, who knows and can appreciate
their worth. My friend has intelligence enough to desire that his wife may have it in abundance. It is your
daughter, gifted as she is, who charms him, whom he
loves and desires, who is necessary to his happiness."
Then followed arguments calculated to allay the prejudice of religion, and Mademoiselle de Tuyll concluded, "If you think well to add a few words as to
the eagerness and passion evinced by the Marquis"
(the Marquis, it may be observed, was far from
evincing these inducements), "you must do that for
yourself. I have already suffered enough in this ridic-
ulous self-praise."

It may be supposed that such expressions as these
could not fail to gratify the paternal pride of Monsieur de Tuyll; the reception of the letter was, nevertheless, icy. Silence reigned at Zuylen. The unfor-
tunate family, always formal, became rigid with
constraint. Monsieur de Tuyll pronounced that the
religious obstacle was, for him, insuperable; that his
daughter would be of age in two years and might
then choose for herself without regard to her parents'
judgment, which must remain adverse. Belle at once

replied that she could not desire, or obtain, her happiness at the expense of theirs. There were long conferences up and down the quiet corridor, long letters written from her locked room, and agitated *pourparlers* in the garden. Belle shows herself at her best in this diplomacy; she abounded in admirable arguments, daughterly duty, and ingenious appeals to the ideal of tolerance which Monsieur de Tuyll, like so many unbending persons, believed to be his rule of life. But her efforts were unavailing: the frontal attack had failed, and the two conspirators fell back upon the strategy of attrition.

Bellegarde was urged to bestir himself, to move the Vatican for the necessary dispensations, and to put a little more passion into his suit. Alas, he has reached the middle time of life "when he can no longer flatter himself with the hope of evoking the ardour of love"; "the solid sentiments to which I aspire," he writes, "lead me to look for a better happiness than can be procured by such transitory intoxication—(*cette agréable ivresse toujours passagère*)"; he trusts to these "substantial feelings" to replace "those of a Corydon." He also trusts that her dowry will be sufficient to pay his debts.

It is on record that Belle read this letter three or four times with great pleasure. The fact is she was entirely free from vanity, and readily admired in others the frankness which she claimed for herself. Nevertheless the feelings which Mademoiselle de Tuyll proposed to herself were not precisely the "substantial" ones of the Marquis. She was entirely explicit on this point. She despatched to Hermenches an immense dissertation—a very masterpiece of frankness—on the exact gradation of ardour which her husband must maintain in order to enjoy a reasonable hope of her fidelity. Nothing could be more just, or more businesslike than her observations. The romantic movement was not yet astir, and Mademoiselle de Tuyll's self-knowledge was veiled in no misty half-lights. There is a quality of truth and goodwill in this honest letter which is of finer style than all the draperies of sentiment.

Monsieur de Bellegarde, on his part, was far less exercised as to his bride's eventual fidelity than upon the score of her formidable intellect. "Those talents which heaven has showered upon your daughter" were far from giving the satisfaction attributed to him by Belle in her draft of proposal; her sense of fact alarmed, her subtleties distressed him; he was in mortal terror of marrying a bluestocking; he wished she would not write him such long letters. "Shorter letters, above all, shorter!" is the anxious advice of Hermenches. "If I have too much wit by half for the Marquis," is Belle's rather crestfallen reply, "let him marry a woman with half my wit. If I am neither to see nor to write to Monsieur de Bellegarde, why does he not take an heiress out of Africa, and leave me to make a marriage by proxy with the Grand Mogul?"

But here, too, she can be sympathetic with the alarm of her suitor. "I find it entirely fitting that the Marquis cannot endure me in the role of prodigy. Nothing in the world is more detestable. My intellectual pretensions were a kind of childhood which I have left behind. I have no longer any desire to exhibit a quality which, if it exists, is sure to show itself sufficiently, and loses half its charm in being advertised. I do not spend ten minutes a month in speculating on what I do not understand, and have come to rest in a very humble and quite contented scepticism. If I am on excellent terms with my own wits, it is because I find they serve so well for every day use, because they can discover amusement in anything and amuse everybody, because they make the happiness of those around me. The Marquis will have no complaints to make on this score. I am laughed at every day, and do not mind anything so long as I am allowed to go my own way with my studies and my writings. But I would not for a throne renounce the occupations of my own room. If I ceased to learn I should die of boredom in the midst of every pleasure and grandeur in the world. If the Marquis cares to read aloud I will learn history while I embroider his waistcoats." "If I bewilder him he has only to tell me to hold my tongue. He will find me now a musician, now a geometer, now a so-called poet, now a frivolous woman, now a passionate one, and now a cold and equable philosopher. Perhaps the diversity will

23

amuse him. The background of my heart he will find always the same." "After all, it is necessary, is it not, to know where Archimedes placed his lever to lift the world?"

Not necessary, certainly, to Monsieur de Bellegarde. His wits did not move in the abstract: they were not even at all serviceable "for everyday use." After a year of courtship he had not yet found out whether Mademoiselle de Tuyll, with her Protestant faith, could become his legal wife, or her children his legal heirs. When Monsieur de Tuyll politely suggested that a little light on this point was to be desired, the Marquis sent him his mother's marriage contract, a hundred pages long, which had no bearing whatever on the subject. This incompetence rather favoured his suit by provoking the mirth of the orderly parent. "When one laughs one is half way to being pleased, and the spectacle of the entire incapacity of a man with whom we are doing business leads one to think of him affectionately and to desire that the affair should reach the conclusion he desires: his incapacity seems to compel us to take charge of his interests." And, in fact, Belle, who makes this observation, took charge of Bellegarde's interests to such purpose that we find her escaping to pay a visit, incognito, to the Bishop of Utrecht in order to settle these technical matters for herself; and—after a fall—she carried a letter for the Pope about her person until it becomes so infected with the balms of a poultice "that it could only serve the Holy Father for a medicament if he should chance to tumble from the Holy See."

The Marquis came to pay his court. He was stiff and polite. "I am on the tight rope with him, we are very upright, very measured in our movements; *point de gambades hasardées.*" He had, as Belle remarked later, "the least persuasive manner in the world; his conscience should be easy—seduction cannot be numbered among his sins." Yet she excused his awkwardness, his coldness, his incompetence; she pleaded his suit, she managed his business. What was the motive of this persistence, one might almost say of this pursuit?

It is most certain the motive was not a worldly desire to become Madame la Marquise. No one was ever more genuinely democratic, by instinct, taste, and conviction than Mademoiselle de Tuyll. All her life she detested the constraints of society. She loved simplicity, and sought to surround herself with simple folk. When the gay Hermenches described to her the delights of a country house party of seventy guests she replied with horror; a dance of Dutch peasants was more to her taste. She held the tenets of Rousseau with the assurance of a *grande dame.* Her brilliance and her reputation would have secured her a great place in the world of Paris: it was precisely the position she did not want. "My desire to see Paris might be chilled, if I were Bellegarde's wife, by the fact that he is too *grand seigneur*, and his family have too many great names. I might have to conform to their grand manner, and I do not like the great, nor the grand manner, nor to conform. My chief wish would be to see Paris on foot, or in a cab; to see the arts, the artists, and the artisans; to hear the talk of the crowd and the eloquence of Clairon. I would make some chance acquaintances whom I should like and some others who would make me laugh. I would pay a big price for the lessons of Rameau, and a week before I left, for the sake of completeness, I would make acquaintance with the hairdresser and the world of fashion."

But if the motive was not worldliness, neither, certainly, was it passion. With the best will in the world she failed to fall in love with Bellegarde. At most, and very precariously, this difficult task might be achieved (so she hoped in her more facile moods) with sufficient encouragement from the Marquis; the encouragement was not forthcoming. Yet passion was eminently part of her scheme. "If I did not love my husband, he would be the unhappiest of mortals. . . . But if I love—if I love! I can do nothing by halves, I am capable of no feeble desires, no limited ambitions"; and this fervent lady proposed to marry Monsieur de Bellegarde, the "unseductive" nobleman whose "more substantial sentiments were to replace those of a Corydon"; and what is more she meant to make him happy.

26

The cause of Belle's persistence lay in her singular egoism. All her other suitors had been proposed to her by her parents, or had come forward of their own initiative; Bellegarde was her own creation, the hero of her private scheme, the puppet of her own conspiracy with Hermenches. He had loomed up, a shadowy figure, which her imagination could shape as it pleased. When the outlines became distinct and forbidding he was already a part of her will; a struggle had been engaged; her egoism was committed; and her reason worked unrestingly to justify her choice.

And Hermenches was involved. Hermenches, her choice, on whom her egoism had fastened even more profoundly, Hermenches the confidant of her unending self-analysis. Truly, as she said, it was "an odd thing to upset heaven and earth, to fight with monsters, for the sake of a tepid marriage." But marriage with Bellegarde meant freedom from Zuylen, a gratifying defeat of the monsters, . . . and a future for this embarrassed friendship. For embarrassed it was. "I fear you may hold too large a part in my thoughts, that I may be forming the habit of preoccupying myself with you too constantly, and to keenly (*avec un certain mouvement trop vif*). I am determined that this shall not happen. What would be the end of it? A passion perhaps, perhaps a rupture. . . . I am convinced my parents will never give a formal consent to this marriage; if the Marquis insists on this point, you and I, Hermenches, will not pass our lives together; you will live in Bellegarde's châteaux without me. What shall we do then with the habit that unites us? Will you be satisfied to write to me all your life, and to see me never? Our letters have been all fire, always ardent and tender: after such letters we need to meet. We shall seek each other out, Hermenches—unless we quarrel—and then beware of passion, of jealousy, instinct, madness, and confusion! If I do not marry your friend, if I think always of you, some day we shall be lovers, unless we are separated to the ends of the earth, or unless you care for me no longer." What is to happen to them, she asks, if she does not marry Bellegarde? What is to happen, one cannot help asking, if she does?

This letter to Hermenches reveals a state of mind in Mademoiselle de Tuyll of a somewhat complicated order; a state of mind which may well have been disquieting to Monsieur de Bellegarde and the other eleven suitors. The cautious Marquis hung back. Mademoiselle de Tuyll was perfectly sympathetic: "I hold to the formula of liberty: every morning the Marquis must wake up with the freedom not to wish what he wished the day before"; and when she dismisses another suitor she is at pains that Bellegarde should not know it lest he should conceive his obligations to be increased. The Marquis availed himself of this liberty to the full: every morning, for the space of about four years, he woke up wishing what he had

not wished the day before. But at last his painful du-
biety gave place to a settled conviction. For this
temperament, these conic sections, this alarming wit,
this unsparing frankness, he was no match. But he
found it very difficult to say so.

Unhappy Mademoiselle de Tuyll! After so many
letters, after so much self-scrutiny and analysis, after
"combats with monsters" and visits to bishops, she
was twenty-eight; and still at Zuylen the cattle
browsed on, the windmills slowly turned, the barges
drifted by; and still she endured the "*privation pé-
nible*" of her unmarried state.

But all this time there had been other strings to
her formidable bow. The King of Prussia, for example, had heard tell of this enchantress. A Dutch
gentleman at his court, Belle said, "used to send His
Majesty to sleep with the story of my charms." The
King "liked this story as well as another," and desired to see Mademoiselle de Tuyll at the Prussian
court. Monsieur le Comte d'Anhalt was to wed the
paragon and bring her to Potsdam. The mother, sister, and friends of the Count were full of this desirable project; the Count himself, if not precisely full,
was at any rate favourably disposed.

The circumstances of this proposal were eminently flattering. The Anhalts, it was said, were to receive back their princely rank; the King took a lively
interest in Belle; he had seen her portrait, and advised her to give up reading Fénelon. The Count was

on the point of starting for Utrecht. He was always about to start. He remained in Germany; the trepidation which Belle never failed to inspire, even at a distance, kept him rooted to the spot. Mademoiselle de Tuyll observed the process of his collapse with an amused detachment. The Count d'Anhalt served very well as a pawn in her matrimonial diplomacy; she threatened her parents with him when they were too obdurate against Bellegarde; she used him as an excuse in order to discourage the ardour of a love-sick cousin; and with complete indifference she watched him gradually vanish over the horizon.

She had, near at hand, a more eloquent admirer, who provided for her—and for us— a richer fund of comedy.

II

ON 6TH AUGUST 1763 A YOUNG TRAVELLER took ship at Harwich; he was bound for Helvoetfluys, on his way to Utrecht. Before boarding the packet boat he took leave upon the beach of his companion, a man of impressive aspect, whom he embraced with tenderness. As the vessel put out to sea, the traveller kept his eyes fixed upon his friend "for a considerable time," while the latter "remained, rolling his majestick frame in the usual manner."

At last Dr. Johnson walked back towards the town and disappeared, and James Bowell was free to turn his gaze seaward and to speculate, as he paced the deck, on the adventures that might await him in Utrecht.

His ostensible motive in visiting that city was to perfect himself in the study of law, and in particular to attend the prelections of Professor Trotz upon the Theodosian Code; but "you may figure," he said, "the many spirited, gay ideas which I entertained," for was he not now a young man of fortune setting out on his travels? Jemmy Boswell, as Dr. Johnson warned him, was about "to whirl in a vortex of pleasure." He promised himself to form the acquaintance of "very genteel people"; his engaging affability would break down the reserve of eminent men in Holland, in Germany, in Switzerland; his person, he felt assured, would prove irresistible to a number of ladies of wealth and fashion.

At Utrecht, accordingly, Boswell took pains to penetrate into the best families, and it was not long before he found himself cordially received by Monsieur de Tuyll. He struck up a friendship with Belle's brothers, and was accorded full opportunity of exercising his charm on Belle de Zuylen herself. He did not realize that his chief weapon was his absurdity. He was fervent, fatuous, and kind. He was dazzled; but he was mindful also of Dr. Johnson's admonitions. His brain whirled in conversation with Mademoiselle de Tuyll, but steadied itself in conversation with the Reverend W. Brown, minister of the local Scottish Church. Boswell was much exercised by the need of squaring Belle's view of life with that of the Shorter Catechism. He would make a convert of her and teach her how to behave; but even in her unregenerate state he could not but admire her fervently. Boswell's fervour, or, it would be more accurate to say, Boswell's vanity, was well imbued with Scotch caution. In the midst of his lyrical outbursts he roundly informed "this charming creature" that he would not wed her, no, not if she had the Seven Provinces for a dowry. At most, Belle reports, "if I become more prudent, more reasonable, and more reserved he might try, with time, to marry me to his best friend in Scotland!" "*Je trouvais cela fort bon*" is her comment; *naïveté* like Boswell's was the shortest way to Mademoiselle de Tuyll's affections. She delighted in his transparent simplicity: here was "frankness"! Here was something to laugh at, to tease a little, and possibly—why not?—to marry.

Monsieur de Tuyll had no fears, or, perhaps, no objections. At any rate Boswell was a constant visitor to the house, and for nine months Belle gently amused herself at his expense. And when, in the following June, Boswell set out to Germany in the company of Lord Keith, the pair promised each other to interchange *de grandes lettres*.

It was not long before Belle received from Boswell an effusion covering seventeen pages. It deserves extensive quotation. "As you and I, Zélide" (he called her by her chosen pseudonym), "are perfectly easy with each other, I must tell you that I am vain enough to read your letters in such a manner as to imagine that you really was in love with me, as much as you can be with any man. I say *was*, because I am much mistaken if it is not over before now. . . . You have no command of yourself. You can conceal nothing. You seemed uneasy. You had a forced merriment. The Sunday evening that I left you I could perceive you touched. But I took no notice of it. From your conversation I saw very well that I had a place in your heart, that you regarded me with a warmth more than friendly. Your letters showed me that you were pleasing yourself with having at last met with the man for whom you could have a strong and lasting passion. But I am too generous not to undeceive you. You are sensible that I am a man of strict probity. You have told me so; I thank you. . . . Is it not, however, a little hard that I have not a better opinion of you? Own, Zélide, that your ungoverned vivacity *may* be of disservice to you. It renders you less esteemed by the man whose esteem you value. . . . I would not be married to you to be a king. . . . My wife must have a character directly opposite to my dear Zélide."

Boswell had no doubt that this pronouncement must have a staggering effect. But he hastened to console her: "You may depend on me as a friend." And then he reflected: "It vexes me to think what a number of friends you have. I know, Zélide, of several people you correspond with. I am therefore not so vain of your corresponding with me. . . . Pray write and continue to show me all your *heart*. I fear all your fancy. I fear the heart of Zélide is not to be found. It has been consumed by the fire of an excessive imagination. Forgive me for talking to you with such an air of authority. I have assumed the person of Mentor. I must keep it up. Perhaps I judge too hardly of you. . . . Defend yourself. Tell me that I am the severe Cato. Tell me that you will make a very good wife."

It is evident that Boswell's disinclination to marry Zélide was not so deep as he pretended. But he must first hear promises of reform and see signs of a chastened spirit. "Let me ask you, Zélide, could you submit your inclinations to the opinion, perhaps, the *caprice* of a husband? Could you do this with cheerfulness, without losing any of your sweet good humour, without boasting of it? Could you live quietly in the country six months a year? Could you make yourself agreeable to plain, honest neighbours? Could you talk like any other woman and have your fancy as much at command as your harpsichord? Could you pass the other six months in a city where there is very good society, though not in the high mode? Could you live thus, and be content?"

Auchinleck . . . Edinburgh; the picture grows distinct. It is a guarded, a scrupulously guarded, proposal. "Could you give spirits to your husband when he is melancholy? I have known such wives, Zélide. What think you? Could you be such a one?"

In other passages he had explained more particularly the grounds of his esteem and disapproval. The balance was nicely held. He accorded her "affection, honesty, and good humour"; he allowed her "genius and accomplishments"; but she lacked prudence. She was the "favourite of nature"; but did she sufficiently practise Art? Art had taught her to play divinely on the harpsichord: could she not learn to modulate the faculties of the mind with an equal harmony?

"Consider, my dear Zélide, your many *real* advantages. You are a daughter of one of the first families of the Seven Provinces; you have a number of Relations of Rank. You have a very handsome fortune, and I must tell you, too, that Zélide herself is handsome. . . . But take care. If those enchanting qualities are not governed by Prudence they may do you a great deal of harm. . . . If you resign yourself to fancy, you will have now and then a little feverish joy, but no permanent satisfaction. I should think you should believe me. I am no clergyman. I am no physician. I am not even a lover. I am just a gentleman on his travels who has taken an attachment to you, and who has your happiness at heart. . . . My dear Zélide! You are very good, you are very candid. Pray forgive me for begging you to be less vain; you have fine talents of one kind, but are you not deficient in others? Do you think your *reason* is as distinguished as your imagination? Believe me, Zélide, it is not. Believe me and endeavour to improve."

Boswell was wrong here. Belle's reason was impeccable; she had too much of it; or, rather, she made such a fetish of the reason that her action was paralysed and her feelings found no outlet. But her reasoning did not satisfy Boswell, for it did not lead her to the conclusion of orthodox piety, nor did it accord, in some essentials, with the verdicts of Dr. Johnson.

"Now, Zélide, give me leave to reprove your libertine sentiments, of which your letters to me furnish several examples. You say if your husband and you loved each other only a little, '*J'en aimerois surement un autre. Mon ame est faite pour des sentimens vifs. Elle n'evitera pas sa destinée.*' I hope this love of yours for another is not destined like that of many a fine lady. '*Si je n'avois ni père ni mère, je ne me marierois point.*' And yet you would have your tender connections. Ah poor Zélide! do you not see that you would reduce yourself to the most despicable of all situations? No, Zélide, whatever men may do, a woman without virtue is terrible. Excuse me for talking so freely. I know you mean no harm, you give way to your fancy. You see, however, whither it leads you, '*J'aimerois assez un mari qui me prendroit sur le pied de sa maitresse. Je lui dirois, ne regardez pas la fidelité comme un devoir, n'ayez que les droits et la jalousie d'un amant.*' Fy, Zélide, what fancies are these? Is a mistress half so agreeable a name as a wife? Is a connection of love, merely, equal to a connection strengthened by a variety of circumstances which have a pleasing influence on a sound mind?"

The name of wife: the name of Mistress Boswell of Auchinleck? . . . But, before Belle could be fitted for this high destiny, she must seriously consider the principles of Christianity. The remainder of Boswell's letter is much occupied with religion, the noblest employment of the mind. As to this "great article" he was very happy, and wrote a fine sentence: "My notions of God's Benevolence are grand and extensive. I puzzle not myself with texts here, and texts there, with the interpretation of a gloomy Priest, or the interpretation of a gay Priest. I worship my Creator, and I fear no evil." "You may say perhaps that you cannot prevent your mind from soaring into the regions of Perplexity: Allow me to deny this. . . . Pray make a firm Resolution never to think of metaphysics. Speculations of that kind are absurd in a man; but in a woman are more absurd than I chuse to express. . . . Think of God as he really is, and all will appear chearfull. I hope you shall be a Christian. But, my dear Zélide, worship the sun rather than be a Calvinist."

"I had sealed this letter," Boswell here adds. "I must break it open and write a little more. . . . I charge you once for all. Be strictly honest with me. If you love me own it. I can give you the best advice. If you change tell me. If you love another, tell me. . . . Answer me this one question. If I had pretended a passion for you, which I might easily have done, for it is not difficult to make us believe what we are already pleased to imagine—answer me— would you not have gone to the world's end? Supposing even that I had been disinherited by my father, would you not have said, 'Sir, here is my portion. It is yours. We may live genteelly upon it.' Zélide, Zélide, excuse my vanity. But I tell you, you do not know yourself if you say you would not have done this. You see how freely I write and how proudly. Write you with all freedom, but with your enchanting humility! *'Je suis glorieuse d'être votre amie.'* That is the style. Is not this a long letter? You must not expect me to write regularly. Farewell, my dear Zélide. Heaven bless you, and make you rationally happy. Farewell."

There is little evidence, beyond this precious document, of the relations between Boswell and Mademoiselle de Tuyll. The reader can form his own opinion of Belle's sentiments: it will hardly be Boswell's. We are told that the pernickety Scot was ill pleased with Belle's easy democratic manner. Belle writes to Hermenches, "I like to discourage all marks of cold respect in those around me, and to have, in place of it, love and consideration. There is no one in this house, except my own maid, to whom I give an order; I have never consented to take the smallest authority, but for my sake all would betray my father and mother. I do not care to be respected: I want people to give me much and to feel they owe me nothing. I do not wish to impose myself but to please. *Boswell trouvait cela fort mauvais.* He would rather see me in full dress, with a flowing robe, long sleeves and a serious air, waiting for his approach before permitting myself to smile. . . . 'How can it be,' he used to say, 'that you do nothing to make yourself respected—you, to whom it would be so easy? . . . Keep all those follies, which you tell to whoever cares to hear them, which are misunderstood and misinterpreted, keep them for me—your friend; say them in English! You should respect the jealousies of friendship; remember that friendship will have its privileges and is hurt to see an equal treatment accorded to all the world. Every one is at his ease with you. It is terrible.'"

"Tout le monde est à son aise avec vous! Cela est terrible!" But when every allowance has been made for Boswell's huge fatuity, it seems certain that Belle regarded him with as much affection as amusement. Mademoiselle de Tuyll had a distinct leaning to ludicrous men; she loved honesty, and readily forgave the ponderous casing in which honesty is frequently enclosed. She had quickness enough for two; perhaps she took a malicious pleasure in bewildering these weighty folk. Bellegarde and Boswell, and later, as we shall see, Monsieur de Charrière, were of this type; the first was an amiable fool, the second a prig, the third a pedant; all three were rigid and circumspect and slow; but each had a disarming honest absurdity. And Belle de Zuylen was still a Tuyll: she could not resist integrity. She had to make love to good men.

It took four years for Boswell's fervour to get the better of his caution. In the interval he travelled, returned to Scotland, and paid court to Miss Blair, "the finest woman he had ever seen," and one who "studied his disposition." But the memory of Zélide haunted him, and at intervals he pondered, long and prudently, on her qualifications to be mistress of Auchinleck. Could she endure Scotland? Could she restrain her levity, and abandon her infidel notions? Would she, above all, look up to him?

He consulted the Reverend William Temple, who was the official confidant of his amorous adventures. He consulted Sir John Pringle, the physician. He consulted General Paoli, who upset him with a vivid account of the ladies of Corsica. He consulted Jean Jacques Rousseau. "During my melancholy at Utrecht," he wrote to Rousseau, "I made the acquaintance of a young woman of the highest nobility, and very rich. I conducted myself in a way to win the reputation of a philosopher. But ah, how deceptive are appearances! If you care to amuse yourself by reading some pieces by this young lady, you will find them in a small separate parcel."

Meanwhile, to Boswell's mortification and astonishment, Zélide had forgotten him altogether. "Zélide has been in London this winter," he wrote to Temple in March 1767. "I never hear from her. She is a strange creature. Sir John Pringle attended her as physician. He wrote to my father: 'She has too much vivacity; she talks of your son without either resentment or attachment.'"

This was unforgivable. "I am well rid of her," he exclaimed to Temple; "you say well that I find mistresses wherever I am; but I am a sad dupe—a perfect Don Quixote."

Then, nine months later, when Boswell had

steeled his heart, came a letter from Zélide, "written in English, and showing that an old flame is easily rekindled." He learnt with delight that Belle was engaged in translating his "Account of Corsica and Memoirs of Pascal Paoli" into French. Boswell's vanity went at once to his heart. "Do you know my charming Dutchwoman and I have renewed our correspondence? and upon my soul, Temple, I must have her."

He had forgiven her at once for her obliviousness. "She is so sensible, so accomplished, and knows me so well, and likes me so much"; and he began forthwith to make his matrimonial preparations. "I do not see how I can be unhappy with her. Sir John Pringle is now for it, and this night I write to my father."

But neither Lord Auchinleck nor the Reverend William Temple favoured the idea of this foreign, flighty, and infidel enchantress. "I find the fair and lively Zélide has no chance for the vote of the Rector of Mamhead. My father is quite against the scheme. . . . However, I cannot help thinking both my father and my friend too severe. Zélide may have had faults, but is she always to have them?" Boswell felt confident that he could mould her to his will, convert her to his religious views, and induce in her manners a touch of haughtiness and decorum suited to his bride. In his mind's eye he pictured her at Auchinleck, parading "the old castle, and when I am to make the superb grotto," she should stand, at once stately and romantic, on "the natural bridge" and pace in long sleeves with a serious air "down the grotto-walk to the Gothic bridge." And his guests should be vastly satisfied and impressed. "Upon my soul, Temple, I must have her."

"I have not yet given up Zélide," he assured the rector. "Just after I wrote you last, I received a letter from her, full of good sense and tenderness. 'My dear friend,' she says, 'it is prejudice that has kept you so much at a distance from me; if we meet I am sure that prejudice will be removed.' . . . Be patient, Temple, read the enclosed letters and return them to me. Both my father and you know Zélide only from me. . . . How do we know but she is an inestimable prize? Surely it is worth while to go to Holland to see a fair conclusion, one way or other, of what has hovered in my mind for years? I have written to her and told her all my perplexity; I have put in the plainest light what conduct I absolutely require of her, and what my father will require. I have bid her be my wife at present and comfort me with a letter in which she shall show me at once her wisdom, her spirit, and her regard for me. You shall see it. I tell you, man, she knows me and values me as you do."

Zélide's answer, unhappily, is not preserved. But its tenor may be judged by its effect on Boswell. He was completely taken aback; so different was it from that other letter, "full of good sense." ("Ah, my friend," he moaned to Temple, "had you but seen the tender and affectionate letter which she wrote me! . . .") "I told you what sort of letter I last wrote to her; it was candid, fair and conscientious. I told her of many difficulties: I told her my fears from her levity and infidel notions, at the same time admiring her and hoping she was altered for the better. How did she answer? Read her letter. Could any actress at the theatre attack me with a keener—what is the word? not fury, something softer. The lightning which flashes with so much brilliance may scorch, and does not her *esprit* do so? Is she not a termagant, or at least will she not be one by the time she is forty? . . ."

Boswell was instantaneously converted to Lord Auchinleck's and the Reverend W. Temple's view. "Indeed, Temple, thou reasonest well. You may believe I was perfectly brought over to your opinion by this acid epistle. . . . I have written to my father, 'I was eager for the Guards and for Mademoiselle; but you have happily restrained me from both. Since then, I have experienced your superior judgment in the two important articles of a profession and the choice of a wife. I shall henceforth do nothing without your advice.' Worthy man! this will be a comfort to him upon his Circuit.

"As for Zélide I have written to her that we are agreed. My pride (say I) and your vanity would never agree: it would be like the scene in our burlesque comedy 'The Rehearsal.' 'I am the bold thunder,' cries one; 'The quick lightning I,' cries another, '*et voilà notre ménage.*'"

So Belle de Zuylen abandoned her translation of Boswell's "Account of Corsica" and announced that she was perfectly decided not to marry him.

Then Boswell hastily discovered in himself a similar decision.

And Boswell reflected. Had he not told her, years ago, that he was a "man of form, a man who says to himself thus will I act, and acts accordingly? In short a man of discipline, who has his *orders* with as much exactness as any soldier. And who gives the orders? I give them. Boswell, when cool and sedate, forms the rules for Boswell to live by."

So, sedately, Boswell attributed Zélide's refusal to his own prudence. He sounded the retreat. And, like a soldier, he obeyed the call.

His wounds were quickly healed. "I am exceedingly lucky," he wrote next August, "in having escaped the insensible Miss Blair and the furious Zélide, for I have now seen the finest creature that ever was formed, *la belle Irlandaise. . . .*"

Would Zélide have given the same answer four years earlier? It is very doubtful. Belle de Zuylen as Mrs. Boswell—truly a charming speculation for English minds! What passages might not have been added to the "Life of Johnson." For Zélide was not one to be silenced by a "Madam, you err!" In the entire "Life" there is no record of the doctor's en-

countering any adversary so formidable as she. His
flagrant unreason would have met at her hands with
a quick justice which no volleys of rudeness could
have parried. Decidedly Dr. Johnson would not have
loved Mistress Boswell. And Zélide? It would have
been a difficult, a heroic case; but—she had to make
love to good men.

These things were not to be. Destiny reserved for
Mademoiselle de Tuyll a much duller, much better
man than James Boswell. Yet England, with its unconventional ways, its leniency to strong character,
was perhaps more than any country her spiritual
home. Already, at Utrecht, she had become the devoted friend of Lord Heathfield (then General Eliot)
and his wife. This gallant warrior, the defender of Gi-
braltar, whose ruddy, testy face Reynolds has de-
picted against the smoke of battle, shared Belle's dislike of form and ceremony, and recognized in her
eccentricity, so suspect to her countrymen, the true
quality of humour which he had imagined to be a
British monopoly. Belle, on her side, was not less en-
thusiastic: "long live the English for their freedom of
intercourse, for that ease of theirs which is not a
manner, not a point of form nor a convention, nor
another kind of constraint as it is with the French,
but true ease, true liberty." The general's wife haz-
arded some "gauche caresses, which contained a
hundred times more true friendship than a French-

woman could have demonstrated with a thousand superlative protestations," and sought to entice her to England with stories of Handel and good beer. A year later the scheme was realized; Boswell's letter to Temple has already mentioned Belle's presence in London. For suitors were at a standstill; Mademoiselle de Tuyll's matrimonial epic was distinctly flagging; the consolations of Plutarch seemed a little threadbare, and even conic sections not what they were. She escaped accordingly from the monotony of windmills, and saw "as much of England as a woman may see in six months."

Her account of British manners at this epoch is brief and distressing. "True ease, true liberty" seen at close quarters, had their disadvantages. "The women," she says, "are reserved and sulky in society: the men expect it. . . . If you are a little gay you find your foot trodden on and your arm pressed when you least expect it by men who are complete strangers; that is, if they are fashionable." Formal society, as usual, she avoided, and at court she could never remember to say "Sir" to the Prince of Wales. She was happier in her "loggings," entertaining rough David Hume to a dinner of plum-pudding and beef.

Mademoiselle de Tuyll, by her own account, made some stir in London life. She put a bridle on her wit; she concealed her deplorable learning; she refused to let Lord March carry her off in his chariot; she was a miracle of tact. But not a single proposal of marriage rewarded this maidenly behaviour. She returned to Holland and took stock of her melancholy situation.

From Zuylen she looked out over the world. The soft-lighted moody sky filled all the picture; the four turrets of the quiet castle pricked small into its unmeasured height; here and there the flat meadows were shadowed with rain, or, across them, the tower of Utrecht Cathedral rose white in shafts of watery sunshine. Near by the slow Vecht flowed between poplars, and below her window the moat ruffled to the wind, or reflected smoothly the image of a bird. All was tranquil; the portcullis in the low gatehouse hung like a toy between the sleep of the trimmed garden with its obelisk and the sleep of the unending fields.

III

ER FIRST THOUGHTS AT ZUYLEN WERE
again of Bellegarde—or, at least, of that
vague personage who in her dreams had the
name of Bellegarde and the features of Hermenches.
"How I wish that, without more ado of letters, so-
licitations, arguments, inspections, and disputes, I
might wake up to-morrow morning in the château of
the Marquis and hear 'Good-morning, Madame de
Bellegarde'; but I have tramped so long a journey to
reach that château that I cannot find strength for another step. I have no better marriage in view: I do
not know what a good marriage means." This is not
in Belle's lively manner; this is, plainly, a last gasp.
The final scene is at hand; it was staged, like another
final scene, in the castle of her cousin, Count Ben-
tinck, at Amerongen. Here, at one end of the great
corridor, lodged Mademoiselle de Tuyll, at the other
Monsieur de Bellegarde. "In the evening he was
brought to my room, and I remembered in a far-off
way the Pope who would not allow him to stay
there." Bellegarde nerved himself for the declaration; no more would he wake up in the morning
wishing what he had not wished; he said it out: "He
was not worthy of her hand." It was the end of four
years' struggle.

Mademoiselle de Tuyll was not precisely humili-
ated by this rejection. An egoist, but an egoist without vanity, she took these things very simply; she rue-

fully considered the waste of ink and paper and midnight oil expended in the self-analysis and diplomacy of four long years, and with a certain bitterness of fatigue she writes to Hermenches: "Never speak to me again of a husband: if I want one I shall know how to find him for myself!"

It is indeed very noticeable that, from this date, the letters to Hermenches begin to lack their old familiar frankness. In place of voluminous intimacy there are dark allusions. "Many strange things are passing in my heart. . . . I do not tell you all I think, nor my half-plans: it is so useless from a distance— one sees things so differently. . . . My star is a strange one! If you were by my fireside I could tell you many things." Then come references to "a man I will not name": disquieting references; embarrassed references; one might almost say, shamefaced references. "If you have seen him, it can only have been in passing; in that case you did not notice him, or you must have disliked him. . . ."

For, all this time, there had been another gentleman in the background; a very quiet, correct, gentlemanly gentleman with a stammer; a gentleman who understood conic sections and had, in fact, come to Zuylen long ago as the tutor of Belle's brothers. Worthy Monsieur de Charrière was one of those characters, conspicuous for simplicity and stiffness, whom it was Mademoiselle de Tuyll's habit not only—and rightly—to admire, but also, from some

occult perversion of her nature to dazzle and to se-
duce. He possessed, she said, "the simplicity of
La Fontaine, a firm and even temper, a just, upright,
and enlightened spirit, a tender and generous heart,
and"—best of all—"a certain clumsiness of mind
and manner, which could be freely trifled with, for
no one ever had less vanity." The first document—
but presumably by no means the first incident—in
this friendship is a letter written by Monsieur de
Charrière in 1766. It will be seen that he shrank from
Belle's encouragements. Braver men than he, in like
case, had done the same. *"Mademoiselle,"* he writes,
"vous êtes inconcevable! Why do you recall to me
memories which you have forbidden me to retain?
How can you say that you are my friend, when you
trouble my happiness by making me see how much
happier I should be if you were something more?
Your sentence on the subject of prudery transported
me in thought to your room: it was midnight, silence
reigned in the house, and we two, alone together,
were talking. You, Mademoiselle, like a physician at
his experiments, gave to your heart and mine now a
greater and now a less degree of heat; you observed;
you reflected; and our feelings were, for you, no
more than so many *phenomena.* . . . Mademoiselle, I
shall come back to Utrecht: in God's name, do not
sit up with me again! Do not show me again so much
goodness, if you have decided not to show me still
more!"

This is a warm letter; but later on, so Mademoiselle de Tuyll relates, the correspondence grew warmer. "We wrote to each other and our letters became more animated. I was alone in the country; there was not a man of interest in the whole land;— our letters became more animated. My correspondent drew near. Now at Utrecht and now at the Hague we spent many days together. The retirement in which I was living, the habit of confidence and liberty which our intercourse had taken—you can imagine where this led. But do not imagine too much; do not imagine all!"

These nicely guarded indications are sufficiently precise for biographical purposes; they enable us to understand what Mademoiselle de Tuyll had in mind when she spoke of "finding a husband for herself" after the flight of Bellegarde. But, as the prospect of marriage loomed up, the ex-tutor began to hesitate and tremble, and his stammer, I imagine, was much in evidence, as also "a certain clumsiness of mind and manner." Now if ever that "firm temper" must get the better of that "tender heart." And, to Monsieur de Charrière's great credit, it did. "He argued," Belle relates, "that it was the very worst project in the world!" "I am but a poor gentleman," he protested, "I have no merits which could compensate for all you would throw away. Your attachment is not of a kind that can be durable. You desire pleasure, and do not know how to obtain it; and you mistake for love what is only a transitory fever of your imagination. A few months of marriage will disabuse you; you will be unhappy; you will take refuge in pretence; and I should be even unhappier than you." Never had Monsieur de Charrière's "enlightened spirit" been more just or more penetrating. In one point only did the sequel disprove his prophecy. Madame de Charrière never took refuge in pretence.

The prudent arguments advanced by Monsieur de Charrière sufficed to allay the experimental enthusiasm of Mademoiselle de Tuyll. She recognized their force; she always recognized the force of any argument. It was certain that Monsieur de Tuyll would obstinately oppose so inglorious a union. She respected the reluctance of Monsieur de Charrière to enter her family on such terms; she genuinely desired his happiness and that of her father. Accordingly, for the time being, like the physician in his laboratory, she gave her feelings "a lesser degree of heat."

Matters were at this temperature when Mademoiselle de Tuyll returned from Amerongen. Her state of mind at this crisis in her life is extremely perplexing and perplexed. She was twenty-eight: an age, which, in the eighteenth century, might well fill a maiden heart with dismay. Her last hopes of the Marquis had vanished; what was to take their place? A marriage of reason, or of inclination? She had thought about it so much that, in her own phrase, she no longer knew what a good marriage meant. She was weary and disillusioned, the prey of conflicting moods; and the morbid activity of her mind entangled each mood in a chain of arguments. She had at different times reasoned herself into love with Bellegarde and out of love with Hermenches; she could reason herself in or out of anything or anybody. What process should she adopt towards Monsieur de Charrière? The dull routine of the great house at Zuylen gave her the vapours. She relinquished algebra and mechanics and applied herself listlessly to painting. But nothing availed to lighten her neurasthenia. The sudden death of her mother threw her into even profounder desolation. "No words," she writes to Hermenches, "can depict the horror in which we are plunged. I can neither read nor write: these few lines have cost me infinite difficulty. I work when I am alone, or I go and cry with my mother's old maid." In this mood the idea of love became "a crime." The melancholy which had always lain beneath the surface of Belle's exuberant life darkened all her thoughts. "If we had Carmelites in this country," she exclaimed, "I would become a nun."

Should she remain single? "*Ah, Mademoiselle, restez comme vous êtes!*" Prince Henry of Prussia had exclaimed at the close of a courtly flirtation. Alas! the single state was not her calling. Had she not admitted that, to her mind, "Virgin-Martyr" was a tautological expression?

The consequence of this state of self-abasement

was truly astonishing. Among the candidates for Belle's hand at this moment was Lord Wemyss, an attainted leader of the Rebellion of '45, who was passing his exile in Switzerland and Paris. This ferocious nobleman was a stranger to Mademoiselle de Tuyll; she merely knew that in the rebellion he had desired to cut off a finger from every English prisoner. In the absence of Carmelite nuns Mademoiselle de Tuyll proposed to accept his offer. It was pointed out to her that Lord Wemyss was violent, despotic, and notoriously dissolute. "No matter," replied the would-be Carmelite, "a being such as I am at present deserves, at the very most, a Lord Wemyss. I should be too ill a gift to make to another." She announced her intention, subject to her father's consent, of marrying him immediately, in much the same spirit as one may enter a convent, with vows of virtue and indifference. "But I will make vows, also, to be useful and industrious if I can. I will ask God for a spirit of reasonable devotion, gentle, indulgent, and charitable, which will serve instead of the pleasures of a lover." As to Lord Wemyss, "Until I have seen him," she writes to her brother, "I can only tell you that his reputation is unfavourable as to his tastes, his pleasures, and his character. It does not matter. No doubt he will not beat me."

The consternation was general. Why Lord Wemyss? Why not, for instance, Monsieur Obdam or Monsieur Pallant? Why not, above all, Monsieur de

Wittgenstein? The last was warmly recommended by Hermenches; he was, positively, "the next best thing to Bellegarde." Monsieur de Tuyll himself asked nothing better. But Belle always made the same answer: "Monsieur de Wittgenstein has a name and expectations; he is good and kindly; why should he be dragged into my destiny? Lord Wemyss, I think, deserves nothing better."

How much of this was due to neurasthenia, and how much to a subtle design, is uncertain. Monsieur de Charrière was in despair. He had met Lord Wemyss, and shuddered at the future which awaited his beloved lady. Trembling and unworthy as he was, might it not be kinder to marry her himself? Monsieur de Tuyll was placed in a similar dilemma. He could not desire his daughter to marry his ex-tutor; but, said Mademoiselle de Tuyll, it must be one or the other, the tutor or the debauchee; "the matter is in your hands," she exclaimed, "choose between these two men, and decide which shall be my husband!" Gentle Monsieur de Tuyll assumed that quiet manner which was "as obstinate as the Pope's mule." He listened to his daughter's pathetic speech without the slightest emotion—and continued to talk placidly of Monsieur de Wittgenstein. But it was Tuyll against Tuyll. Belle's fighting spirit was once more awake, and she meant what she said. "I shut my eyes," she says, "as one does before a danger one is bound to confront." She sent messages to Lord Wemyss who was now in Paris; she learnt that he was waiting for a decoration. This touched her democratic scorn, and would seem to have angered her more than the amputated fingers. "I am told," she observes, "that a very small German prince has already decorated him with a very large star; truly these are puerile ambitions for an attainted lord! Will such a man be my husband?" Lord Wemyss, on his side, was only too ready for the honour. He wrote "that Mademoiselle de Zuylen must send him an exact specification of her property; that he would do the like for her with regard to his own; and if they found that, together, their fortune would enable them to live on the footing they desired, Mademoiselle de Zuylen had only to name any city in Flanders or the Low Countries where she desired to give him a rendezvous for the marriage." Here at last was a suitor who, so to say, came up to the scratch! Meanwhile, in the general alarm, other friends—Monsieur de Welderen, Monsieur de Salgas—intervened to plead the cause of Monsieur de Charrière. Monsieur de Tuyll, most properly outraged at the tone of Lord Wemyss's letter, began visibly to relent; he wavered; he gave in. But Monsieur de Charrière himself, as his prospects suddenly brightened, was seized with the old panic. "Could you not," he stammered, "could you not remain, just a few months more, as you are? What are a few months, what is a year, at the price of a whole life?"

And Fate, which was to claim from both these lovers that full price, for some months longer held the
balance in suspense. Mademoiselle de Tuyll had a
last access of frankness; again she detailed to Monsieur de Charrière the alarming catalogue of her
faults. On this subject she could be vivid and convincing. No wonder that Monsieur de Charrière repeated with an almost wounding insistence: "Remember that I will respect your liberty to the last
hour: up to the last moment of the last ceremony you
are free!" No wonder that Mademoiselle de Tuyll
found herself saying, "He loves me without illusion
and without enthusiasm; he is just and sincere to a
painful degree. Yet how can I live without him?" For
here was the point of pathos in this tragic comedy:
their justice, their honesty revealed to the two lovers,
who knew themselves so well, their perilous unfit-
ness; yet she loved his "justice," he loved her "honesty of heart." And so Fate's balance was weighted,
and wavered, and fell.

They were married at Zuylen on 17th February
1773. The Dutch festivities of the occasion were
homely and cheerful; the menace of Lord Wemyss,
the sincerity and simple goodness of Monsieur de
Charrière, had reconciled all hearts. Mademoiselle
de Tuyll described the occasion: "*A minuit et demi,
ils s'allèrent tous coucher, les uns avec leur femmes,*
etc." Toothache tormented the bride, and Monsieur
de Charrière felt ill by reason of the punch. A touch

of cruel realism! Truly, Mademoiselle de Tuyll regarded all feelings, impartially, as "phenomena." Was she not right? Would it not have been kinder perhaps to marry that undeserving nobleman, Lord Wemyss?

IV

So it was that Mademoiselle de Tuyll at the age of thirty, and to the astonishment of Europe, became Madame de Charrière; and she who had scorned the dullness of Holland prepared to settle down with the ex-tutor, his aged father, and two spinster ladies of his family, in the sleepy old manor at Neuchâtel. It was the amazing marriage. "Who could have thought it?" observed the Statholder; and the King of Prussia and the other august personages, who had watched the career of this Dutch divinity, made similar reflections. But one man —the friend who knew her best—was not surprised. "It is precisely the kind of idea," said Hermenches bitterly, "which was to be expected from a head like yours."

No one was in a better position to judge the workings of that curious mechanism, Belle de Zuylen's head, than Constant d'Hermenches. For twelve years she had revealed every cog and pulley of the machine to him in the cold rays of her self-analysis. And he was right in discerning that this fantastic marriage, with its air of free romance, had been determined far more by her head than by her heart. Only after much debate had her intellect decided that this was a case where her feelings might be given a considerable "degree of heat." Monsieur de Charrière was good, and she heartily approved goodness; he was intellectual, and could read history with her; he was simple and unworldly, and she knew that she was too un-compromising for society, and that the world had nothing to offer which it was worth her while to take. Chafing under the restraints of Zuylen she had accustomed herself to look to marriage as the gate of freedom: Monsieur de Charrière, most timid and self-effacing of men, could be trusted not to interfere with her in thought, word, or action. All these were sound calculations. Proximity and that "painful privation" had done the rest. She gave her imagination free rein, accordingly, and decided that Monsieur de Charrière was "the most tenderly loved husband in the world."

But Belle's self-analysis was here at fault. She was kindly, but not tender. Nevertheless to the task of tenderness she now addressed herself with all the force of her overflowing energy, and with all the processes of her sane intellect she fostered that gentle emotion. Her mind would never admit that she had more claims on happiness than another; eagerly she placed her vitality at the service of those less vitally endowed. It was her fate to be always surrounded with companions less alive than herself. *"Ici l'on est vif tout seul!"* At Zuylen she had done her best to galvanize the passive Tuylls; she would do the same for her grave and orderly husband; and in her exile she would teach the Swiss infants of the village (passive, no doubt, and orderly once more) according to the precepts of Rousseau, and the dictates of reason.

Tenderness! Madame de Charrière's excellent heart approved the quality, and she made her arrangements accordingly.

The first months of the marriage were spent at Utrecht, and at Paris where Madame de Charrière's delight was to take painting lessons from La Tour; then in September 1774 she confronted the lifelong monotony of Neuchâtel.

The family of de Charrière belonged to the small nobility of the Pays de Vaud. The grandfather of Belle's husband, after suffering banishment from Berne on a charge of quietism, had settled in 1701 in the manor of Colombier, which was to be Madame de Charrière's home until her death. Colombier is a characteristic Swiss country house of the seventeenth century, built round a spacious court and surrounded with vineyards; and here a senile father-in-law and two middle-aged sisters-in-law awaited the arrival of the bride. Mademoiselle Louise, an amiable old maid, was to be seen all day in the large walled garden, tending the flowers and vegetables, while Mademoiselle Henriette, less amiable, looked after the housekeeping. It cannot have seemed a very promising *ménage* to the restless, independent, and uncompromising Belle. The society on the shore of the lake had little to offer by way of enlivenment, and Madame de Charrière, who despised the glitter of Paris, was hardly likely to be beguiled by the mundanities of Neuchâtel. She had chosen the simple life, and she set herself to live it in all good will. Since Mademoiselle Henriette ruled the saucepans and Mademoiselle Louise was the mistress of the cabbages, gay Madame de Charrière, the admired of princes, the "favourite of Nature" and the ornament of art, betook herself to washing clothes at the fountain in the court. Was it not healthier, she asked, than to talk—and to listen to talk—all day long? And had not Nausicaa, another favourite of Nature, done something of the kind? And in the evening they played at "Comet," an excellent game, but not the best for Mademoiselle Henriette's temper; or Madame de Charrière would cut silhouettes out of black paper; and Monsieur Chaillet, the interesting young pastor, would drop in and read his sermon on "Spring."

In such a life, so isolated from the world, all turned on the human relation between Monsieur de Charrière and his wife. Would that equitable spirit and equable temperament, which Belle had admired in her brothers' tutor, suffice for the needs of her vital and grasping and withal so disillusioned spirit? It would seem that for a while she was happy. But, for these early years of Belle's married life, we are dependent largely on conjecture. That correspondence with Hermenches, to which we owed so close a knowledge of her thoughts, now lost its intimate character and soon ceased altogether. His refusal to return the unguarded letters of her youth did not create a breach yet shook Belle's trust in the honour of her confidant. Hermenches, on his side, was equally disappointed. He had dreamed for Belle a future of worldly brilliance, a career worthy of the gifts he had admired and done so much to form, a life in which they should be friends and perhaps something more than friends. And instead, his disconcerting pupil insisted on describing to him the merits of her humdrum husband, and the charms of washing linen at the pump.

In vain he remonstrated with her "that princess of the Odyssey had not brains like yours. I cannot abide you in the role of *lavandière*, or as a kitchen-garden nymph!" She seemed perverse in her rusticity. Colombier was but a few miles from Ferney: she might at least have known Voltaire, and shone in the little court which surrounded the philosopher. Moreover Hermenches was intimate with Voltaire, and Ferney might have taken the place of Bellegarde's château as a meeting ground. But Madame de Charrière was obdurate. "Your last letter," she replied, "was dated from Ferney. You desire me to be there. I cannot desire it. Voltaire is a scoundrel with brains. I will read his books; I will not go to swing my censer!" The answer is characteristic. Madame de Charrière was the enemy of all pretensions, whether intellectual or social. She would be a Circe to a simple man; she could not flatter a great one. She "did not like the great, nor the grand manner, nor to conform," and she would not swing a censer. Nevertheless, unconsciously, for fifteen years she had swung a censer to Hermenches; she had made him her *alter ego* and confided to him every scene of the drama which her mind and senses perpetually played. It was the greatest compliment an egoist could pay. And now that she would pay it no longer the friendship ceased, and Hermenches passed out of her life.

But the role which Hermenches relinquished was to be assumed, years later, by his own nephew, Benjamin Constant. It is to him we must turn for an authentic testimony to the melancholy truth. "It was at this time" (1787), writes Benjamin in the "Cahier Rouge," "that I became acquainted with the first woman I had met of a superior intelligence, and one who had more of that quality than any I have ever known. Her name was Madame de Charrière. She was a Dutch woman, of one of the first families of that country, and had made a great stir in her youth by her wit and the eccentricity of her character. At more than thirty years of age, after many passions, of which some had been sufficiently unhappy, she had married, in spite of her family, her brothers' tutor, a man of intelligence and of great fineness and delicacy of character, but the most cold and the most phlegmatic it is possible to conceive. During the first years of their marriage his wife had greatly tormented him to impart to his temperament a movement equal to her own, and the sorrow of only achieving this end at rare moments had very soon destroyed the happiness she had promised herself in this to some extent unequal match."

This, then, had been the end of that Dutch-Swiss idyll! *Sa femme l'avait beaucoup tourmenté pour lui imprimer un mouvement égal au sien.* Alas for good, methodical Monsieur de Charrière! Had he not prophesied it? He had done his best; just in all things, he had meted out his endearments with punctual exactitude; and behold—his wife was unhappy! He had read history aloud to her; and she complained that he read too well, too distinctly. He had been equable and wise; and she called him phlegmatic and meticulous. He had sympathized with her solitude, he had encouraged her to pass the winter in Geneva; and there, in a manner which was not *ordentlyk* at all, she had fallen in love with a good-looking, but in other respects most inferior young man! . . .

For so it had befallen. Benjamin's laconic narrative continues: "A man much younger than herself, of very mediocre parts, but handsome, had inspired in her an extremely lively attraction. I have never known the details of this passion; but what she told me of it, and what I have learnt from others, sufficed to inform me that it had procured her great agitation and unhappiness; that her husband's displeasure had troubled her domestic life; and that finally, the object of her passion having abandoned for her another woman, she passed through a period of the most terrible agitation and despair."

To the end of her days Madame de Charrière would never allow this lover's name to be uttered in her presence. The future has kept her secret, and the researches of the historian have failed to disclose his identity.

"But this despair," Benjamin concludes, "turned to the advantage of Madame de Charrière's literary reputation, for it furnished the inspiration of the most charming of her works. The story is entitled 'Caliste,' and forms part of a novel published under the title of 'Letters from Lausanne.'"

This observation provides the clue which enables us to fill the gap of years dividing the correspondence with Hermenches from the correspondence with Benjamin. These two men, the uncle and the nephew, had in common a gift of psychological sincerity which answered irresistibly to Madame de Charrière's inveterate craving for "frankness." To each in turn she revealed herself with a dry intellectual delight which for her nature was so intense as to replace the glamour of sentiment and entail the ardour and ultimate bitterness of veritable passion. As a girl she took Hermenches for father-confessor; in middle life she was to fill this role for Benjamin, twenty-seven years her junior, and an egoist as accomplished as herself. In the interval between these two friendships she made the world her confidant, and disclosed in a series of brief novels, dryly and without self-pity, the progressive disillusion of her life.

These four novels are the "Lettres Neuchateloises" (1784), the "Lettres écrites de Lausanne" (1785), its sequel "Caliste" (1787), and "Mistress Henley" (1784). From their pages one can reconstruct all that is essential in Madame de Charrière's life during these years: her attitude to the provincial world she had chosen for her environment, the pathetically ludicrous anti-climax of her married life, and something of the profound pain—elsewhere so jealously guarded—of her unhappy passion for the *inconnu* at Geneva.

The actual plot of the "Lettres Neuchateloises" is not autobiographical, and for that very reason it is thin and somewhat uninteresting. Madame de Charrière, whose touch on whatever she had experienced was unerring in truth and sincerity, lacked inventive imagination and took little pains to rectify the defect by any care of elaboration. Everything in the "Lettres Neuchateloises" which is drawn from observation—the social background of the Swiss lake —is on the contrary admirably delineated. Her quiet descriptions of the worthy citizens of Neuchâtel, their incessant talk of the vintage and the price of wine, their heavy wit, their young ladies' somewhat self-conscious gaiety, their fine distinctions between one class of bourgeois and another, are caustic yet

convincing. But they were hardly calculated to pro-
pitiate the goodwill of her neighbours.

To the worldly Hermenches, warning her that she
would find by the lake a petty provincial community
of backbiters, she had retorted with her instinctive
kindliness, "I will find means to please them: I
should be like them if I occupied myself with their
faults." But, when her intellect had taken stock
of her surroundings, she held aloof, it is true, from
the gossip of the town, but, "boredom became my
muse," and she inflicted on the community as a whole
the satire which her neighbours reserved for one
another.

"When one depicts from the imagination, but
with truth, a flock of sheep" (she writes later on in a
letter), "each sheep sees his own likeness, or at least
the likeness of his brother. That is what happened at
Neuchâtel, and people were angry." So angry were
they that Madame de Charrière was practically excluded from their society and lived in almost complete solitude at Colombier.

Insensibility to criticism was a conspicuous trait in
Madame de Charrière's nature. She who judged herself coldly and unpityingly could always accept the
criticism of others with good-humoured irony and
detachment. But, prisoner as she was within her own
ironclad personality, she was quite unable to conceive the sensibility of others except as an irrational
and ludicrous foible. Hence in all her speech and ac-

tions we find justice and generosity, but also a certain unconscious cruelty. Human weakness, of which she had little, was an object to her for astonished speculation merely. Of the niceties of tact she perceived the uses as little as she experienced the need.

So "people were angry"; the little circle at Colombier became still more restricted. The pastor, J. Chaillet, "Servitor of Jesus Christ," came regularly enough, because as he remarks in his diary, he counted on a steady source of income from Monsieur de Charrière's small skill at piquet; and, moreover, Zélide, who loved to shower material benefits on those around her, clothed his children and fed him with capons.

A few other neighbours came and went. Courtly old-fashioned M. du Peyron from Neuchâtel wrote her his daily letter or paid his prosy call. François Chaillet—*le grand Chaillet* he was named to distinguish him from the pastor—lounged in from long botanical walks and rested his lazy giant body and smoked his pipe. Mademoiselle Moula, very demure and rather affected and altogether modest and maidenly, remained for long visits and practised her accomplishments, cutting silhouettes of the company out of black paper and teaching Madame de Charrière to do the same. Monsieur de Charrière played host; his old father had died in due course, and now he was master of Colombier; punctiliously he stuttered awhile with his guests and then buried himself

70

in his books; and then Madame de Charrière, if she was in a good mood, stayed patiently answering platitudes with her wisdom and her wit.

So Zélide lay, lost to the world, like a bright pebble on the floor of the Lake of Neuchâtel. Life: she had schemed for it, and reasoned about it; for life's sake she had rebelled and argued and endured; and now life was this. A discarded play it seemed, without plot or plan; an old, unfinished, ill-written play.

Meanwhile there was a marked decline in Madame de Charrière's health. After her death it was determined that she had suffered since girlhood from an internal malady. The strong stoicism of her nature, the propensity of her will towards action and gaiety, the masculine curiosity of her intellect, all these contributed to combat the mood of black depression, to which at any pause in her activity, she fell a prey. But it is clear that the routine of the life at Colombier and the negative, unresisting smoothness of her husband's temperament were like a perpetual pause which no activity of Madame de Charrière's could fill. She wrote her novels; she shut herself up and composed operas; Mademoiselle Louise and Mademoiselle Henriette, reposing from their useful tasks, would hear the sound of Madame de Charrière's harpsichord at unseasonable hours. But in spite of every effort of distraction, it was remarked that the lady of the house was not happy—that she was, as the observant young pastor records in his diary, "most romantically unhappy" ("so like myself," he adds in his microscopic handwriting; for had not "J. Chaillet, Servitor of Jesus Christ," incurred a reprimand from the Venerable Synod for an excessive intimacy with one of his flock?); that her health and air of abundant life were steadily declining and that she constantly complained of the vapours. She took the waters at this and that resort; she made friends at Strasburg with Cagliostro and was much encouraged by certain yellow drops of his prescription. It is noteworthy, in passing, that Madame de Charrière, no lenient judge of shams and charlatans, had a tender spot for Cagliostro, and defended the character of the great adventurer with considerable warmth. But her melancholy grew upon her; her egoism, bereft of its cheerful buoyancy, took on an air of hardness; her thoughts hung round the mediocre and faithless young man at Geneva whose name might not be spoken, and it was noticed that when the party beguiled the evenings at Colombier with the excellent game of "Comet," Madame de Charrière would forget to play the nine of diamonds, and methodical Monsieur de Charrière, who forgot nothing, or observant Pastor Chaillet, who noticed everything, would win the round.

So Pastor Chaillet watched Monsieur and Madame over the card table, and noted the little incidents that meant so much, and pocketed the little winnings, and went home and wrote in that diary, which resembles those curios where the Lord's Prayer is written on a threepenny bit and seems to our eyes an epitome of his furtive little nature.

He had seen her when she arrived as a bride; she had been an egoist then, but still with so much *bon-homie* and spirit as to make her seem less a selfish human being than a symbol of life itself. Do what she would, she gave more than she took; the sparks from her fire—that glow in her which "could warm the heart of a Laplander"—shone for all alike. But the change which the pastor attributed to the lover at Geneva had its source deep in Belle's nature. Already at Zuylen her reason, cold and destructive, had been making its sceptical comment. Already, there, moods of despondency had alternated with vital gaiety; and health, the mainspring of the mechanism, had begun to give way. Already she had begun to depend on stimulus from outside; and mistaking the stimulus she needed she had reasoned herself into marriage with Charrière; her mind, ceaselessly revolving the problem of her own happiness—in the possibility of which she yet never long believed—had seen in that marriage a loophole of flight from the fast closing cage of her own egoism. And even as she took the step she had cried out against its irrevocableness.

And now Monsieur de Charrière was in truth a very monument to the indissolubility of marriage.

Year in, year out, he displayed, like a good Swiss clock, the same meticulous correctness, the same unchanging regularity. On the even dial of his face no emotion could be discerned. He spoke, in order to control his stammer, with an inhuman, a clock-like distinctness. There he sat between his two sisters, always accurate, always courteous, always reasonable, always there. To Madame de Charrière he may have seemed like some relentless, impassive mechanism, timing, registering, and remorselessly exhausting the counted hours of her life. "No one object," she had cried out as a girl at Zuylen, "can ever satisfy all the activity of my soul." Poor Monsieur de Charrière, an object buttoned up in rectitude and girt about with circumspection, was hardly likely to furnish a proof to the contrary. He did not satisfy all—more and more it became doubtful whether he satisfied any— of the needs of Madame de Charrière's soul.

He knew it. It was no use hoping that he could satisfy her; he lived beside her, and watched himself dwindling in her mind. There had been love, or "a certain degree of temperature" which his poor thermometer could not register, and then pain, and then a dull pain, and then not even a pain but a dullness only. He had sunk to that, and he knew it well. He looked at his quiet sleepy manor house, yes, undoubtedly that was dull, too, for so gifted a wife. He cherished a hope that the winters at Geneva might work miracles, perhaps, in that sunny apartment he had found, Rue Beauregard, all hung with Aubussons. And now Geneva was a subject they both avoided, and the figure of the *inconnu* with his stupid good looks seemed woven into the very tapestries. At any mention of the Rue Beauregard Pastor Chaillet distinctly observed, at both ends of the table, a wince.

Pastor Chaillet comes and goes and has little conversations in undertones and takes his notes. There is a world of meaning in Mademoiselle Henriette's tight lips. Mademoiselle Louise, on the other hand, abounds in sighs of sympathy and bright, brief exclamations of hope. But the pastor is not very encouraging to Mademoiselle Louise. He reminds her that Madame de Charrière has no principles, no faith, and can expect no happiness. "She has certainly brought none," says Mademoiselle Henriette, with a snap. "*Mais . . . mais*," intercedes Mademoiselle Louise: it is her favourite word, and implies a firm belief that black clouds have silver linings. "It will end badly," concludes the pastor.

And once or twice, of a summer evening, after losing a little money at piquet, Monsieur de Charrière, usually so cold, will open his heart walking with Chaillet in the garden: "*nous parlions de nos femmes, . . . d'amour . . .*" Yes, Monsieur de Charrière has unburdened himself at last, notes the pastor in his microscopic diary. And Madame de Charrière? Pastor Chaillet sees no loophole there. The thoughts of Madame de Charrière, sitting alone, are hidden behind dark battlements of reserve.

Solitary, she craved for solitude. She went up to the hills, to Chexbres, where instead of the stammering prudent speech of her husband, she could listen to the cow bells and the crisp sound of the wind in the apple trees. He left her there, hoping in his poor shut mind that the high air and the green fields would bring her back to peace. And, at last, he ventured to pay her a visit, driving up one hot day through the August dust. He said little: he was determined to say little; for he knew his way of enunciating was all wrong, and he had vowed never to speak of his feelings. But when he got home he wrote: "I have seldom been so sad as when I left Chexbres. Your air of friendliness to me at luncheon, several affectionate words you spoke during my visit, and the evidence you yet gave of an opposite disposition, the pity I felt for you, the longing to see you back soon at Colombier, and the fear that this would not be for our mutual happiness—all this was seething in me, and gave me a swelling of the heart and a desire to cry which I had difficulty in restraining. . . . I thought it best to distract myself by talking with the driver." And he added "something which I have for a long time resolved to tell you, namely that

I find many of the faults you have named in me disagreeably evident in my sister Henriette, which helps me to understand your thought, and to forgive it."

And so, on the smooth slopes of Chexbres Madame de Charrière wandered alone, trying to think of Rousseau and contemplating the vacancy of her life; and in the vaulted parlour of Colombier Monsieur de Charrière sat dumb and contemplated his sister Henriette. Yes, he added, "her manner of enunciating when she speaks or reads with care is insupportable. She reduces everything to general maxims; she sees a particular case only in relation to conventional morality; she has no single simple or genuine sentiment," and in fact, "I see in her my own caricature." And with tears in his eyes he forgave his wife's impatience. He sat; and the room filled with dusk.

And as he sat he thought of a book which was then at the printers, his wife's last book, "Mistress Henley," which he himself had copied out for her. And again an image formed dreadfully in his mind—an image of himself. For his wife's last book was autobiographical. No one could mistake it. The sketch was Charrière to the life.

The origins of "Mistress Henley" are sufficiently amusing. Here, once again, the lot of Madame de Charrière is linked with the Constant family. Monsieur Samuel de Constant had published a book

77

called "Le Mari Sentimental"; his elderly hero, Monsieur Bompré, marries a young wife and is driven to despair and finally to suicide by her interference with his habits of life. The interferences are trivial, and relate to his dog, his furniture, his acquaintances: it is a study in cumulative irritation. The book had a quick success. "All discontented husbands," Madame de Charrière tells us, "thought themselves Monsieur Bompré, and marvelled at their own resignation," and one wife, whose husband had died after a year of unhappy marriage, thought it necessary to publish a kind of *pièce justificative*, signed by the Mayor and local officials, to attest her innocence, with ludicrous insistence on the difference of detail in the two cases.

The society of the lake was diverting itself with this incident when Madame de Charrière determined to enter the controversy with a counter-thesis: that a husband from sheer excess of virtue may make life intolerable for his wife. This time there was no doubt as to the identity of the protagonists; no one at Neuchâtel failed to recognize the hero and heroine of her tale. "Madame," wrote a friend, "has not I think painted herself as flatteringly as she might quite justifiably have done."

But precisely here lay the art of Madame de Charrière's story. By putting the heroine, that is herself, always slightly in the wrong, through impatience or quick temper or lack of judgment, and the husband unfailingly and unforgivably in the right, she awakens the sympathy of every reader. The story is, as Mistress Henley says, "a pack of little things." Here is a typical scene:

"My room was upholstered in stripes; very dark green velvet separating panels of hand-tapestry, worked by Mr. Henley's grandmother. Large armchairs, vastly inconvenient to move, but excellent for sleeping in, embroidered by the same hand, together with a monstrous hard sofa, completed the furnishings of the apartment. My angora used to sleep without any respect on the old armchairs and get caught in the antique needlework. Mr. Henley had already placed her gently on the ground several times. Six months ago he came, dressed for hunting, to bid me good-bye in my room, and saw my cat asleep on an armchair.

" 'Ah!' he exclaimed, 'what would my grandmother, what would my mother say if they saw?' . . .

" 'They would undoubtedly say,' I replied with warmth, 'that I ought to make use of my furniture in my own fashion as they made use of theirs, and that I ought not to be a stranger even in my own room; and from the time that I complained to you of these heavy armchairs and this gloomy tapestry they would have prayed you to give me other chairs and other hangings.'

" '*Give*, my dearest life!' answered Mr. Henley,

79

'does one *give* to oneself? Does half of *oneself give* to the other half? Are you not mistress here? Formerly all this was thought very fine. . . .'

" 'Yes, *formerly*,' I replied, 'but I live here now.'

" 'My first wife,' continued Mr. Henley, 'liked this furniture.'

" 'Ah, good God!' I exclaimed, 'would that she were still alive!'

" 'And all this for a cat to whom I have done no hurt!' said Mr. Henley, with a sad and gentle look, a look of resignation; and he went away.

" 'No,' I cried after him, 'it is *not* the cat. . . .' But he was already far away, and a moment later I heard him tranquilly giving some orders in the yard, while he mounted his horse."

The lady is "in the wrong, always in the wrong, in the wrong in everything." "I brought no happiness here, and I have found none," is the author's *cri de coeur*; and when, at last, Mistress Henley writes this letter to her husband, is it not Madame de Charrière who speaks?

"Sir. You observed, I trust, yesterday, how much I was ashamed of my excessive warmth. Do not think on this occasion or on many others, the merit of your patience and your gentleness to have escaped me. I can assure you that my intentions have always been good. But to what use are intentions, unrealized?

"As to you, your behaviour has been such that I can discover nothing to blame in it, however much

I may sometimes have desired to do so in order to justify my own. You have, however, been guilty of one error; you did me too much honour in marrying me. You believed—and who would not have believed?—that a rational woman, finding in her husband all that renders a man pleasing and respectable, and in her situation every honourable enjoyment, would not fail to find also happiness. But I am not a rational woman, and we have both discovered it too late."

Monsieur de Charrière admired his gifted wife. With placid devotion he ministered to her needs as he understood them; and it was his habit neatly to indite the fair copies of her literary works. We learn from a passing reference that he suffered from writer's cramp. Did that strange, that too-fixed expression of benignant calm still illumine his features while he copied this sentence from the opening of her tale: "Mr. Henley will not be recognized; he will doubtless never read what I have written; and, even if he should read it. . . ." Yes, if he should read it, would that loosen his rigid muscles; could that help him to understand?

Surely, if the gods have pity as well as laughter, they shed on Monsieur de Charrière, dumbly transcribing these lines with his cramped fingers, a shining tear!

V

BUT THE GODS, WHO LOVED NOT THE FAULT-less wheels of Monsieur de Charrière's mind, had long been more congenially engaged. Near by, at the parish church of St. Francis at Lausanne, on 14th November 1767, while Monsieur de Charrière was still winding his will to the stroke of matrimony, an infant had been presented for baptism by the name of Benjamin, son of Juste Constant de Rebecque, an officer in the Dutch service, and of Dame Henriette de Chandieu, his wife. Round that cradle the ironic powers had gathered; on this infant as he grew they had showered all their favourite contradictions. They gave him ambition and self-mockery; they made him impulsive yet sceptical; an enthusiast, yet aloof. Conscious of his dual nature, at war in himself and with the world, he learnt to hide the sincerity of a saint behind the poses of a mummer. He seemed of all men the most eccentric: yet understood, as few have done, man's universal motives. He perched in the world like some strange bird of exotic plumage, thinking human thoughts.

He was born to perplex the pedants and confound the moralists, who still to-day write volumes to explain *"le dédoublement Constantien"*: he was designed, consequently, to perplex and confound Monsieur de Charrière, to shock his propriety, to scandalize him by every disorder, to fascinate him by

sheer astonishment, to borrow his money, and to en-
gross and torture the heart of his wife.

Decidedly, Madame de Charrière had a taste for
the Constant quality. Hermenches and Benjamin—
first the uncle, now the nephew: between these two
pictures hangs the Portrait of Zélide.

The friendship between Madame de Charrière
and Benjamin Constant is still to-day, as it was to
Sainte Beuve, the central interest of her story. A tradition, fathered by Sainte Beuve, has presented her
as Benjamin's evil genius. Evidence, inaccessible to
Sainte Beuve, has weakened this view, which was
never a penetrating one; and the further we enter
into the two natures the less justified will it appear.
In any case no opinion can fairly be formed without
a clear image of Benjamin's character as it was before
the "fatal influence" of Madame de Charrière came
into play.

An eccentric father and a still more eccentric
education had already gone far to complete the native oddity of Benjamin. Father and son were both
deeply imbued with the Constant heredity of self-
consciousness, self-mockery, self-torture. They were
estranged by their very similarity, and bound together by the pity of their own estrangement. The father hid his timidity behind a heavy smoke screen of
sarcastic reserve; the son, behind the exploding fire-
works of his brilliance, nervously concealed the

timidity he had inherited from his father. In flight from themselves, they could do nothing for each other.

Benjamin, in the "Cahier Rouge," has recorded his first sense of this situation:

"Unfortunately my father's conduct was dignified and generous rather than tender. I was fully conscious of all his right to my gratitude and respect, but there was no confidence between us. There was something ironic in his turn of mind which went very ill with my character. I was at an age when I only asked to be allowed those simple enthusiasms which remove the soul from the sphere of the commonplace and inspire in it the scorn of surrounding objects. I found in my father not a critic but a cold and caustic observer who at first would smile with compassion and soon conclude the conversation with impatience. I do not recollect during my first eighteen years having ever passed an hour in conversation with him. His letters were affectionate, and full of reasonable advice; but no sooner were we face to face than there was something constrained in him which I could not explain to myself, and which reacted on me most painfully. I did not know then what timidity was. I did not know that even with his son my father was timid, and that often, after having waited for some signs of affection which his apparent coldness had seemed to forbid me, he would go away, his eyes moist with tears, and complain to others that I did not love him."

Yet, in the sequel, Benjamin was to give abundant proof of natural affection, and years of his life were to be devoted to defending his father from the disasters which were to shower on the colonel's proud and saturnine head. And the timidity which Benjamin "did not then know" he was later to recognize as the key to his own meteoric behaviour.

Meteoric, also, was Benjamin's education, and by no means calculated to inspire a confidence in human nature or affairs.

His mother had died a few days after his birth. "My birth," he says, "was the first of my misfortunes." The colonel, long absent on regimental duty, entrusted Benjamin to a series of fantastic tutors, whose services were punctuated by irruptions of the angry soldier. With the first of these preceptors Benjamin entered into a characteristic conspiracy to invent a new and secret language, of which the alphabet, vocabulary, and grammar were successively evolved: by this ingenious expedient the child Benjamin, at the age of five, found himself possessed of a precocious command of the rudiments of Greek. But after this hopeful beginning, Juste Constant bore the boy away to Brussels and handed him to the charge of "an atheist of mediocre ability, but an accomplished libertine," who for the greater convenience of his pleasures took the child to live in a house of ill fame. Becoming tardily aware of Benjamin's lamentable situation, Juste arrived hot foot from his regiment—*"mon cher papa, qui arrive"*—and, with every mark of natural indignation, transferred his son to the care of a music master. This worthy man had nothing to impart, and Benjamin, now aged eight, shifted for himself in a neighbouring library, where, from eight to ten hours a day, he consumed all the novels and irreligious tracts of the time. Once more, a cloud of dust: *mon cher papa, qui arrive*; Juste has discovered a new tutor, extremely fair-spoken, extremely expensive, Monsieur Gobert. For a year Benjamin worked with Monsieur Gobert: his work consisted in transcribing a history by Monsieur Gobert of which Monsieur Gobert required several copies. But he addressed himself to this task with such scant attention and executed it in so disastrous a handwriting, that at the end of the year he had not advanced beyond the preface; and grave public scandal having meanwhile been excited by Monsieur Gobert's private morals (tutors were all alike), Juste arrived once more and removed his son with expressions of customary force. He selected, by way of successor to Monsieur Gobert, an unfrocked monk, who subsequently committed suicide. Juste at once conceived a profound contempt for this "good and spiritual man of feeble character"; and as Benjamin, at thirteen, was observed to possess the intellectual gifts of a man of thirty, his father bore him off, at this tender age, with the intention of placing him in the University of Oxford. Notwithstanding his son's precocity, which was universally attested, Juste decided, upon a closer view of this seat of learning, that the boy was too young. Benjamin was swept back to the Continent. More tutors were selected, no more fortunate than the first; Juste abandoned the tutorial system, and Benjamin at the age of fourteen entered the University of Erlangen.

These incidents of Benjamin's boyhood do much to explain his disillusioned mind and nervous sensibility. Yet even in these early years everyone remarked on the candour and sweetness of disposition which accompanied his precocious sagacity, and on the uncanny detachment which was compatible with the highest spirits.

His letters at this period give proof of this most curious quality: a double life in which mind and temperament are completely severed. He is barely twelve when he writes: "My *étourderies* upset all my plans. I wish there were some way of preventing my blood from circulating so fast and giving it a more cadenced movement. I have tried to see if music could produce this effect; I play *adagios* and *largos* fit to send thirty cardinals to sleep, but by some magic or other these slow airs always end by becoming *prestissimo*. The same thing happens when I dance. The minuet always terminates in a few jumps. I think, my dear grandmother, that this trouble is incurable and will prove impervious to reason. There should be some spark of reason in me as I am a few days over twelve, yet I cannot detect its empire. . . . Do you know, my dear grandmother, that I go into society twice a week? I have a fine suit, a sword, my hat under my arm, one hand on my chest, the other on my hip; I hold myself very straight and appear as grown up as I can. I look and I listen, and thus far feel no envy for the pleasures of the fine world: the people look as if they had no great love for each other. At the same time the gaming table and the gold I see spinning excites me. I would like to win some for a thousand needs I have, though others treat my needs as fancies."

Constant is here in miniature. The child Benjamin looks down on himself in the ballroom, and knows just how he appears and how he feels, and speculates on what he will become, and realizes already that the faculty of reason—with which no child surely was ever more precociously endowed—will have very little control in the matter: the detached reason, relentless and quiet in the midst of the cataract, taking no responsibility, experimenting on itself, uncoloured by self-pity or self-praise, concerned merely to take note of the adventure and to record, if need be, the catastrophe.

In other childish passages his more serious interests are foreshadowed, Homer already "gives me great ideas"—forty-eight years later he published "The History of Polytheism"; and there are pages which charmingly prove the warmth and native loyalty of his affections. But already the gambler glints from Benjamin's infant eye—"*le jeu et l'or que je vois rouler me cause quelque emotion*"; and already the Don Juan expresses himself with an infant relish: he is ten when he writes, "I sometimes see here an English girl of my own age whom I prefer to Cicero and Seneca. She teaches me Ovid, whom she has never read and never heard of: I find the whole of him in her eyes. I have written a little novel for her. I send you the first pages; if you like you shall have the rest."

Possessed of these whimsical attractions, Benjamin no sooner arrived at Erlangen than he was given a position at the court of the Margrave of Anspach and found himself at fourteen the favourite of the Margravine. "As I did not hesitate to say everything that came into my mind, laughed at everybody and maintained the most absurd opinions, I was no doubt a sufficient diversion for a German court." His dual nature, at once grave and fantastic, showed itself: he threw himself into philosophers and historians at the University, and piled up gambling debts at court. At fifteen, for the greater dignity of his position and the edification of the Margravine, he selected a mistress. "I am probably the only man," observes Benjamin, "whom this woman actually resisted," but the reputation thus acquired and the exasperation of the Margrave "consoled me sufficiently for having to pass my time with a lady who had no attractions for me, and for enjoying no rights in return for my expense." The wrath of the Margravine was implacable; Benjamin was disgraced, once again Juste Constant intervened, and father and son set out forthwith for Edinburgh.

Here, Benjamin tells us, he passed the happiest eighteen months of his life. Edinburgh was at the height of its European fame; professors were great men, and philosophy was in fashion. Benjamin, with intervals for the culture of the wild oat, studied Greek and History with ardour, and the records of the Speculative Society attest his force and assiduity as a debater.[1] His themes were characteristic: the Influence of Pagan Mythology; universal toleration; duelling; Ossian; the emancipation of women. He spoke English fluently with a Scotch accent. Mackintosh recalls the young Baron de Constant, a Swiss of singular manners and powerful talents, as a leader among the brilliant students of that day.

Constant's philosophic and moralizing bent, coupled with a native wildness, were better suited to the zest of the northern city than to the rococo pleasantries of a German court. But new gambling debts beset him; he retired to Paris in a mood of dissipation; Juste Constant's chariot once more rattled up

[1] v. Rudler, *Jeunesse de B. Constant.*

the street, and Benjamin in taciturn penitence was removed to Brussels.

Here he first conceived the plan for that history of polytheism which was to haunt him all his life. Later on, when he had reacted from the Voltairean bias of his youth, he wrote: "Had I been less ready to abandon myself to all the impressions which were agitating me, I might in two years have achieved a very bad book and acquired a little passing reputation which would have satisfied me greatly. My *amour propre* once engaged, I should never have been able to alter my opinions, and the first chance paradox would have fettered me all my life. If laziness has its disadvantages, it has also some solid rewards."

Nevertheless, not laziness, but another frailty which he shared with the ancient gods, was the true obstacle to the progress of the history of polytheism. Two liaisons, at this period, are recorded by Benjamin in a manner that throws light upon his character. Of the first he wrote, twenty-six years later, "Madame Johannot has a place in my memory apart from all other women. My relation with her was brief, and amounted to little, but the tenderness she gave me was paid for by no agitation and no suffering, and at forty-five I still feel gratitude for the happiness I owed her at eighteen. Her days ended in conditions of great sadness. . . . I was living in Paris, in her neighbourhood, not knowing she was there, and she died within a few steps of a man who has never heard her name spoken without the profoundest emotion, thinking herself abandoned and forgotten by the entire world." The object of the second friendship, to which, after a feverish bout of mythology, Benjamin shortly abandoned himself, was Mrs. Trevor, wife of the British Ambassador at Turin. The affair is recounted in the "Cahier Rouge," and exhibits Benjamin in his usual mixture of *gaucherie* and histrionics, wildness and timidity, irony and suffering, with suitable duels and beating of his head against the wall. The fact is that in Benjamin's dual personality the histrionic element was an impetus with which his mental demand for sincerity was perpetually at war. Women evoked the actor in him, and played upon that; but he reserved a lasting gratitude for those who freed him from the exasperation of his own comedy by piercing behind the mask.

This is the picture of Benjamin, from his own confessions in the "Cahier Rouge." But behind this harlequinade waits the author of "Adolphe," a book that could not be grounded save in suffering, nor conceived save in the loneliest sincerity of contemplation, nor constructed save by the clearest and most pitiless art.

How could it be otherwise, with the nature so sensitive, the blood so fast, the mind so cold and aloof? Grave projects, fame, and the war for liberty; great books, the history of religion; tender and continuous human loyalties; all these. But try as he might to play life's tune *adagio maestoso* it ended—like those early exercises—an agitated *prestissimo*; and however courtly the minuet, he must needs destroy the figure by some access of violence, some frozen gesture of timidity, some sudden impulse of escape; yet all the time the measure of his mind beat time with unde-flecting justice.

The world saw the fantastic figure he presented. It was reserved for Madame de Charrière, who alone never criticized his extravagance, who encouraged his perversity, to see the sincerity which lay beneath.

Had she not memories of herself at Zuylen as a clue?

Such was Benjamin Constant in 1787 in Paris. And hither, in her last escape from Switzerland, came Madame de Charrière, drawn by the magnet, called destiny, which lures like to like.

VI

FOR IT HAD DAWNED ON MONSIEUR DE CHAR-
rière's mind that his wife needed a change. Decidedly after fourteen years a real change was
indicated: fourteen years since the oak gate of Colombier had first clanged behind Zélide; fourteen
times the lime tree in the court had shed its leaves,
and still Mademoiselle Louise purred and Mademoiselle Henriette's narrow eyes watched, and Monsieur de Charrière sat between his sisters with folded
hands. Her health was worse. Cagliostro's yellow
drops had lost their efficacy. "If your spirit were
calm," wrote Monsieur de Charrière, "your body
would soon be cured." But how to cure that brood-
ing spirit? From those snatches of solitude at
Chexbres, at Payerne, she came back and was soon
as melancholy as she was before, sitting shut up there
in her room, writing books.

Books—how terribly quickly she wrote them,
how slowly he copied them out, and how sad they
made him to read! Her last book, the "Lettres de
Lausanne" with its sequel, "Caliste," had made him
sadder even than "Mistress Henley." For in this last
revelation of his wife's mind he could read between
the lines all that he had lost. But of himself he found
no mention, no apology, not even a caricature.

The first part of the book is a slender story, told in
a series of letters from a mother to her child, Cecilia.
Here was his wife as he had loved to think of her—

her honesty, her kindliness, her witty good sense, her
deep instinct to protect. For was she not always protecting—protecting Pastor Chaillet, whom she did
not like, protecting tiresome Mademoiselle Moula,
and making, later, a veritable crusade of protection
about that illegitimate baby of her maid? She seemed
to protect everyone but her husband: he felt himself
to have fallen, somehow, through a hole in her mind.
But now, in these pages, he discerned the full force
of an unmentioned sorrow—his wife's childlessness.
In these letters of a mother to her daughter he saw
his wife imagining, creating for herself, the relationship she lacked, giving to it all the wisdom, the care,
and intimacy she felt herself capable of bestowing.
He saw that here too she had been profoundly
thwarted. Life had given her no Cecilia: it had only
given her a Mr. Henley. And, very slowly, Monsieur
de Charrière understood; he understood more than
his stammering tongue could express.

But the thing that hurt most was to read "Caliste."
Not that "Caliste" is autobiographical in the same
sense as "Mistress Henley." The structure, the incidents, the plot, are for once wholly imaginary. The
story is put together with all the romantic machinery
so dear to the eighteenth century. We have infants
confused at birth, fraternal devotion and bereave-
ment, consolation from a woman virtuous and talented but unjustly disgraced, paternal severity, filial
submission, feminine meekness, tragic and final sep-

aration. But into this box of battered marionettes Madame de Charrière has breathed, even through the lips of the unsympathetic and Werther-like hero and narrator, her own sincerity, her own vigour, and, for once, her own poignancy of emotion. The parting of Caliste from her lover retains its pathos even to-day.

There can be no doubt that she saw herself as Caliste. We know from Benjamin that the story "drew its inspiration" from the love affair at Geneva, and she herself said, "I have never had the courage to re-read 'Caliste': it cost me too many tears to write."

Caliste is Madame de Charrière's hidden self: or, if you will, her anti-self. Caliste is made up, singly and limpidly, of all those emotions she knew she could have lived by, and had not. Zélide, at Zuylen, had sometimes revealed them ("But if I love . . . if I love" she had written to Hermenches, the words starting like a jet from a smooth rock); but she had lost herself in the maze of her own mind: her sceptical and mocking reason. Yet, in the "Portrait of Zélide," the features of Caliste are there behind the mask she was resolved to wear, and wore till the mask stiffened upon the face. Here, for once, she told it out. Caliste dies: it is the only one of her tales that can be said to have a conclusion. She wrote "Caliste," and never re-read it.

But Monsieur de Charrière, copying its pages, understood. Once more the hateful *inconnu* at Geneva rose before his eyes. But that was not the sting. The sting was in the pity of it. He knew that he had never elicited the Caliste in Madame de Charrière, that he never could, that he would not know how to deal with her if he did. He contrasted the woman in the story with the woman in his life, and his heart, within the case which contained him, tightened with pity for himself and for her.

So Monsieur de Charrière concluded that a change was necessary. She had spoken of going to Paris—to Marseilles—to Italy. Where should they go? Where, in a well-ordered world, do unhappy people seek and find distraction? He understood that Paris was the place devised and set aside for just these occasions. And had not wise Monsieur de Salgas declared that his wife was "born for Paris"? In Paris she would forget her solitary preoccupations; she would find people to talk to in that brilliant way of hers, she who had grown so silent. New people . . . strange oddities, such as she had always liked. There were far too few of them at Colombier. All sorts of people. People like Benjamin Constant. . . . He sat, fitting the dates, calculating the expenses, weighing the pros and cons; and destiny, which lures like to like, looked over his shoulder. He assented:— Paris.

Monsieur de Salgas was wrong. Madame de Charrière did not like Paris. "Paris," she wrote, "has no seduction for me. I see more here to disgust and re-

volt than to enchant me." Later she added, "I found
the Parisians cruel rather than gay. . . . Their carni-
vals are forced and revolting and joyless. . . . They
would crowd round some unlucky madman and try
to enrage him, and then rush off to see a fellow creature broken on the wheel." But, as on her first visit,
she found her own distractions, studying counter-
point with Tomeoni, writing minuets, and buying an
occasional work of art. "I find occupations which
depend on no one but myself, and get amusement
enough in my own odd way." As for society, she felt
as little desire to shine in it as before. She found the
epigrams false, the gallantries dull, and the compliments stale. She was looking for something else.

And one evening—at Madame Suard's it may
have been—she found it. There in a crowd of indifferent frilled or starched figures stood young Constant, the nephew of Hermenches, and therefore, if
for no other reason, interesting to her. An interesting
figure, and decidedly an odd one. Tall, lanky, red-
haired, short-sighted, untidy, given to stumbling over
the furniture, and yet with a style to him, an air, an
assurance—or was it a shyness? Human, at any rate,
and very different from the smiling purveyors of stale
gallantries that Madame de Charrière spent her time
in avoiding. She watched him alternating between
sudden silences and unlooked for extravagances of
speech; he seemed always to put himself wilfully at
a disadvantage, yet his grey eyes were mobile with an

alert comprehension: it was clear they missed nothing of the game. It was not long before they sought out the gaze of Madame de Charrière, who missed very little either.

The Constant magnet is at work. Twenty-seven years ago she had singled out Hermenches in the duke's ballroom at Utrecht: "with our first words we quarrelled, with our next we were friends for life." The Constant quality, what was there about it that made her go so straight to the point, that evoked such queer intimacy,—an intimacy flowering into fantastic shape almost before it was planted? For a moment Madame de Charrière is Zélide once more: those fourteen years at Colombier have dropped out: her imagination, hovering between the uncle and the nephew, has a hundred fancies at a flash. But here is something more real and convincing than Constant d'Hermenches. Benjamin is not the professional *charmeur*, but something at once wild, witty, and abashed, by turns easy and ill at ease—bewildering to himself, half conscious only of his charm. But Madame de Charrière has already defined that charm exactly; already she is prepared to unravel Benjamin's personality to its last complicated thread.

They talked; they met again; they talked; they spent whole nights talking. To Benjamin, Madame de Charrière was, above all, the first person who understood him. He was tired of being alone, behind the scenes of his own play. He needed someone who could hold the prompt book for him; someone who should intuitively comprehend his nature, sensitive, complex, affectionate behind its mask of mockery. He was the tragic harlequin, profoundly solitary. He had never known intimacy: certainly he had not found it among the mercenary and *louche* pack of tutors who had alternately alarmed and stultified his childhood, nor in the kindly uncomprehending old grandmother who had been his early confidante away there at Le Desert; nor yet in his histrionic love affairs with women who had no perception of the nature of his mind; least of all had he found intimacy with his saturnine father. The colonel's understanding was like a lash.

He needed someone who should not quarrel with his fantastic extravagance of conduct: who should see it for what it was—the result of heredity, the outcome of an abnormally kindled imagination acting on the hair-trigger of his temperament. Above all he needed a friend who should recognize that his mind, living—compelled to live—in a series of unreal situations, was hungry for reality, impatient of shams.

Zélide at Zuylen had been in much the same case. And the impatience of shams, after fourteen years of Mademoiselle Henriette's platitudes and her husband's moralizations, had become a positive congestion. It was on this ground that Madame de Charrière and Benjamin first met.

"The turn of her mind delighted me," wrote Benjamin long afterwards; "we spent whole days and nights in talk. She was very severe in her judgments on everything that surrounded her. My own nature was full of mockery. We suited each other perfectly. But it was not long before we found ourselves in a relation of more real and essential intimacy. Madame de Charrière's outlook on life was so original and lively, her contempt for conventional prejudices so profound, her intellect so forceful, her superiority to average human nature so vigorous and assured, that for me, a boy of twenty, as eccentric and scornful as herself, her company was a joy such as I had never yet known. I gave myself up to it rapturously."

Madame de Charrière seldom went to bed before six in the morning. By day she slept and Benjamin got into mischief. At night they talked about it. To talk! the joy of it. Benjamin's talk is unforeseen, swift like summer lightning. Before a word is well said he has understood you and answered you out of some new quarter of the sky. Poor Monsieur de Charrière, ankle deep in a bog, with him you move a yard at a time to a fearfully foregone conclusion. After fourteen years at that pace, here, indeed, is something like motion! The joy of swiftness—of leaving out all the intermediate steps—of never knowing where you are going to arrive—of touching the earth so lightly and disdainfully! So the time passed on silver wheels, while the light of dawn dimmed the guttering candle.

Monsieur de Charrière sits on his chair in the background for the first few hours of the night, and says little. He listens while the universe of accepted things seems to tumble about his ears. Prudent reserves, logical demurrers, shape themselves in his brain; but before they are well formulated the talk is away, it is out of sight, it seems to be about something else: not *ordentlyk* at all, this conversation. He had better not try to take part; he will sit by, and raise no objections. What indeed, he keeps reminding himself, is there to object to? For here, by miracle, is Zélide coming back to life before his eyes. "How right to bring her to Paris," he reflects, as he takes his taper at midnight and leaves them to their breathless rejoinders. "And what in the world will they be talking about now?"

Well, as like as not, they have left abstract subjects: Benjamin has dropped for a while his plans for the history of polytheism, his views on philology, his ideas on free will. The universe is being given a rest; and he is recounting, perhaps, his conversation with a pompous and sedate personage of fifty, how he had made fun to him of their common acquaintance, and how after an hour of this, "do not permit yourself to think," he had concluded, taking the elderly gentleman gravely and a little shyly by the hand, "that because I have mocked at our friends in your company I have entered into any engagement not to mock at

you in theirs; I warn you most solemnly that I have
made no such treaty."

Impossible young man! Madame de Charrière
watches him, her head thrown back, with that whimsical challenging look in the eyes—one eye a little
different to the other—as La Tour had drawn her
twenty years ago. Madame de Charrière is looking
twenty years younger.

Yet she is in constant pain. The doctors have pre-
scribed opium. But Benjamin is the one unfailing anaesthetic. She has made him a present of her bottle
of opium. . . .

But, more likely, Benjamin is telling her of his
worries, of his gambling debts, of all the money he
owes to Madame de Bourbonne. "She plays cards
day and night, everywhere, in her carriage, in her
bed, in her bath. . . ." Impossible not to lose to Madame de Bourbonne. In fact, these gambling debts
have landed him in an absurd, a quite terrible, situation. It had fallen out like this. The thing was urgent; he could not raise another penny, and he be-
thought himself of his friend, kind Madame Saurin,
the philosopher's wife, sixty-five years old, who had
been a beauty once, and was now the only person to
remember it. And Benjamin (he is ashamed to confess it) had sat down and written to the good dame,
explaining the crisis, and saying he would call next
day for the money. And next day, accordingly, he had

presented himself at her house. How could he know
that his letter had miscarried? that she had never received it? that she had not the dimmest idea why he
was there? After a long and embarrassed avoidance
of the subject, he had ventured with downcast eyes
on a shamefaced circumlocution. "You will have
been surprised at my step . . . only your affection and
kindness to me encouraged it . . . your silence makes
me fear I have offended you . . . my admission was
torn from me by an irresistible impulse of confidence. . . ." And, as Madame Saurin remained
speechless, Benjamin had raised his eyes to her look
of blank incomprehension. "My letter? . . ." "But I
have never received it." Hastily he had sought to re-
trieve the situation. "Never mind about the letter.
There are moments when a man loses his head. I
value your friendship. Please forget what I have
said." "No, no," Madame Saurin had exclaimed.
"Why do you doubt my heart? I must know all. Go
on. Go on!"

And at this, Benjamin recounts, she had covered
her face with her hands, and was trembling in all her
body. Suddenly he realized his words had been taken
for a declaration of passion. "This misunderstand-
ing, her emotion, and a large bed of red damask at
my side threw me into inexpressible terror." He had
made cruel haste to cast the crude light of truth: "I
have been gambling. . . . I wrote to you for money,"
and had become frozen with pity and shame, stand-

ing there transfixed. Silently, automatically she had counted out the money. Silently, automatically he had received it. They parted without a word.

Mortifying, agonizing episode. . . . But what a story for Madame de Charrière!

And then, no doubt, Zélide, with a tear for poor Madame Saurin, would laugh as she had not laughed since those far, immoderate days at The Hague, when the dowagers had looked round exclaiming—*"une demoiselle . . . cela!"*

And, at the sound, Monsieur de Charrière wakes up in the next room, and looks at his watch, and shakes his night-capped head. Six: and the day breaking. After all there is no harm in it. Benjamin is twenty-seven years younger than his wife, he calculates, turning his head to his comfortable pillow, and—yes, he cannot deny it: he likes that impossible young man. And again he sits up, and listens:—the old laughter of Zélide! Yes; Paris is working its cure.

But this happy *ménage* cannot last. It is time for another incursion by Colonel Juste de Constant de Rebecque. Had not Benjamin's whole career been snapped at intervals by the sudden impulses of this perturbed parent? Always in the very midst of the chapter there is a cloud of dust on the horizon, and the sound of that chariot is heard.

This time, however, the Colonel did not arrive. He merely sent an ultimatum. He had heard of the gambling debts, and he sent one of those well-merited letters of reproach, declaring that he could only allow Benjamin to remain longer in Paris on condition of his doing something sensible. Something sensible, for example, would be to marry young Mademoiselle Pourrat, who possesses—the colonel has been informed—among other merits a thoroughly sensible income.

Benjamin had always been a prey to the filial instinct; the image of his father never failed to work powerfully upon his nerves. He was fond of him, and afraid of him. Discussion with the colonel had always been out of the question. Obedience and flight were the only two methods which the son could venture to employ. It appeared that Mademoiselle Pourrat was sixteen years of age, and extremely pretty; and it was not long before Benjamin was entirely persuaded that this was a case for obedience. There were, it is true, alternatives: quite a number of ladies in Paris had a wife for Benjamin in view. But his mind was clear: for beauty no one could compete with Mademoiselle Pourrat; and, for all the rest, there could only be Madame de Charrière.

Monsieur and Madame de Charrière were sympathetically inclined to the match. Monsieur de Charrière, in particular, welcomed this manifestation of sensibleness—of something *ordentlyk* after all in his wife's friend. Unluckily it transpired that Mademoiselle Pourrat was already engaged to someone else. And here the matter should have ended.

But this was exactly the kind of difficulty that stimulated Benjamin's dramatic sense, especially when Madame de Charrière was looking on at the play. He had reason to think, moreover, that Madame Pourrat, the girl's mother, was not unfavourably disposed to his suit.

Yet instead of availing himself of the mother's good will, Benjamin must needs adopt a more picturesque approach. He wrote the young lady "a beautiful letter" based on the entirely imaginary assumption that she was being forced into marriage with his rival against her will by the cruelty of her parents; and he proposed an elopement.

The young lady, says Benjamin, dutifully showed this letter to her mother, replying that it was not a proper kind of letter for her to receive; and Madame Pourrat had sufficient humour, and enough benevolence towards Benjamin to assume a pretended ignorance. She allowed Benjamin to see her daughter repeatedly and alone; but, says Benjamin, "on these occasions I was overcome with timidity; I never spoke to her but on the most insignificant topics, and I *made no allusion whatever to the letters which I daily addressed to her* or to the passion which inspired them."

And so the comedy proceeded. "Anyone would have imagined that I was writing to an unhappy victim who had implored my help and loved me as passionately as I imagined myself to love her; and in fact my chivalrous proposals were all made to a very reasonable little individual who cared for me not at all. . . . But I had taken this road and nothing could induce me to leave it."

Benjamin was by this time recognizably in love: it merely required a sufficiently *outré* situation to provoke that. He continued to talk quietly "on insignificant subjects" with the daughter, to confide his passion to the friendly ear of the mother, and to pour out these nightly written proposals of elopement, urging the young lady—who did not love him—to fly from the bondage of a parent—who desired nothing better than this match.

And (here is the significant point) Benjamin adds: "in all this I was in perfect good faith with both the mother and the daughter; but I had embarked on this course with the one and the other and, for the devil, I could not dislodge myself from the line I had taken up."

Over this situation, surely, Madame de Charrière laughed the whimsical laugh of Zélide, and threw back her head with the La Tour gesture, while Monsieur de Charrière shook his in perplexity. For here was the purest exhibition of Benjaminism—*le dédoublement Constantien*, as modern psychologists have pedantically described it; here was the pure, the delightful article. The boy was suffering; he was in the devil of a mess; the chances of a happy termination were rapidly vanishing; the conversations with Mademoiselle Pourrat on insignificant topics were a torture; he was deeply distressed at his disloyalty to Madame Pourrat; and yet he had no choice; he never in his life had any choice, never was master of any situation; and any scene had to be played out at its own pace to its own conclusion, even if the *adagio* became *prestissimo*, as in those minuets of his infancy.

But at night, in those interminable conversations, what an account he could give of it all—what detachment, what delicate analysis, and what humour! Madame de Charrière became tender at the thought of that clear mind, that ultimate integrity—the one human being she had known who could never take himself in.

Benjamin, on his side, encouraged by her understanding, passively accepted his absurd predicament. But the climax was at hand. For Madame Pourrat had a lover, Monsieur de Sainte-Croix, and Monsieur de Sainte-Croix looked askance on these long talks, *tête-à-tête*, between Madame Pourrat and Benjamin, the scope of which he minsinterpreted. One day he interrupted them with a violent scene of jealousy. Madame Pourrat, at this, proceeded to explain the situation in all its improbable detail. As she spoke Benjamin awakened sharply to the humiliating absurdity of his position as it must appear to Monsieur de Sainte-Croix, who had by no means got the amused appreciative eye of Madame de Charrière.

He felt the situation to be quite suddenly intolerable; his mood of terror was upon him; and before Monsieur de Sainte-Croix had time to make a caustic or a sympathetic observation, Benjamin had laid his hand on the bottle of opium—Madame de Charrière's opium—which was still in his pocket. He imagined its properties to be more deadly than they actually were. His mind, watching the scene, as usual, from another world was limpidly clear: it argued distinctly: "if the bottle kills me, that will conclude my hopeless business; if not, Mademoiselle Pourrat cannot but be melted towards a man who was ready to put an end to himself on her account. . . ." And, "accordingly I swallowed my opium." But Monsieur de Sainte-Croix was upon him in a flash: he was in time to upset half the bottle; acids were administered, and other remedies to which Benjamin submitted rather from a sense of embarrassed politeness than a desire to survive. And, on this, enters Mademoiselle Pourrat, dressed for the opera; and Benjamin, so far from referring to that suicide which was to have melted her heart, politely offers to accompany her to hear the first performance of the "Tarare" of Beaumarchais.

Who can it be—it is asked—who is keeping Madame Pourrat's company in such merriment—the life and soul of her box? It is young Constant, so witty and bizarre, but a great intellect: his history of polytheism will be a great book. No one, not even little Mademoiselle Pourrat laughing up at him, is aware that he committed suicide an hour ago—that strictly speaking he is dead.

All the same, here, thought Madame Pourrat, the business had better end. And grave Monsieur de Charrière will give just the right note of decorum. Monsieur de Charrière accordingly was summoned. He interviewed demure Mademoiselle Pourrat upon the subject of her affections. No, she had not the slightest feeling for Benjamin Constant; she was extremely well satisfied with the matrimonial arrangements made for her before he arrived upon the scene; and as for his letters they had been very puzzling: in fact, since he has never once referred to them in any conversation, they have been very puzzling indeed.

Monsieur de Charrière walked back with this information to his wife and Benjamin. If he had detected the smallest sign of any inclination—even the very slightest—he would (he insists) have pleaded Benjamin's cause. For he could not help liking Benjamin.

But his wife and Benjamin Constant were in their merry mood; they did not take Monsieur de Charrière's tidings at all tragically. For, says Benjamin, "all the time I was performing these follies, the person who genuinely absorbed my heart and my mind was Madame de Charrière herself; and, talking with her through the whole night, in the midst of my attempts at elopement and my endeavours at suicide, I would forget, in her company, my father, my debts, Mademoiselle Pourrat, and the whole world."

If the fantastic turn of Benjamin's life in Paris be a fault, and not, as Madame de Charrière was disposed to see it, a picturesque scattering of cerebral wild oats, there is no doubt that she was partly responsible for it. "My conversations with Madame de Charrière were like a ferment in my brain," writes Benjamin, and again, "I am convinced that, had it not been for my talks with Madame de Charrière my conduct at this time would have been much less mad," and again, "the talk of Madame de Charrière, its force and flow and eccentricity, kept me in a kind of spiritual intoxication which contributed not a little to all my follies at this period." But he adds, "she had, I am convinced, no idea of the effect it would produce in me. . . ." No, she quite simply enjoyed him, sympathized with him, and watched, with a detachment as complete as his own, the explosive experiments he could not help conducting in the laboratory of his own temperament.

How well she understood it! Years ago she had written of herself to Hermenches: "my soul is like a little ball on the end of a long string; at the least shock it makes extraordinary movements and goes flying up to the ceiling, one way first, and then the other." The description fitted Benjamin perfectly: a bright ball on a string, wildly oscillating. Was it not tempting, was it not irresistible to give the ball an occasional pat? Was it not delightful to observe that, however far it swung, it came back to a centre, and that the centre was herself?

Colonel Juste de Constant looked at the matter differently. The gyrations of his gifted son were, in his eyes, preposterous and expensive. His brow was darkening. He had heard of the failure of the marriage project with Mademoiselle Pourrat; the gambling debts were still piling up; perhaps, too, he mistrusted the influence of Madame de Charrière. In any case it was time to recall Benjamin, and to admonish the son he loved more than anything in the world with a few biting sarcasms.

Accordingly, he despatched fat Monsieur Benay, a lieutenant in the regiment he commanded, with instructions to proceed to Paris to lay hands upon the prodigal and to conduct him to his father's presence, immediately and without fail, there at Bois-le-Duc. They can travel back, he adds, in the *berline*: he had brought Benjamin to Paris in it and left it there.

But Benjamin had long ago sold this carriage to pay a creditor. So the first night is spent in showing Monsieur Benay the sights of Paris, and dining at the Palais Royal. And there alone at the next table is sitting the Chevalier de la Roche Sainte-André, Benjamin's friend—learned chemist and great gambler at Madame de Bourbonne's pool. Benjamin whispers to him, aside, of his predicament, his recall, his fears of his father; and, while he whispers, he hears himself saying that there is never any way with the colonel except flight or obedience, and he would rather run away. The chevalier manifested little interest in the matter. "Where shall you go?" he asks. "To England," Benjamin hears his own voice saying, on the spur of the moment, by way of a reply.

And in this manner the decisive acts of Benjamin's life were normally determined.

He has thirty louis, borrowed from Madame de Charrière. But how to get rid of Monsieur Benay? The fat lieutenant never left his side. The preparations for their departure are complete. The prodigal son is stowed away in a one-seated carriage—the only vehicle to be found—with the vast bulk of Monsieur Benay perched between his knees. The driver has orders for Bois-le-Duc.

But fate always lent an encouraging finger to Benjamin's escapades: fate, which had miraculously caused all two-seated carriages to disappear from Paris, which had made the road so bumpy, and the lieutenant so fat. After half a mile of physical torture Monsieur Benay can bear it no longer: he groans aloud, and decrees a return to Paris.

And that night, with thirty louis in his pocket, and a parcel containing a spare shirt and his slippers, Benjamin creeps down stairs; the sleepy concierge pulls the string of the latch; and he is free. Had not Madame de Charrière talked intoxicatingly, nights ago, on the beauty, nay, the very duty, of independence?

Step by step, before sunrise, the arrangements for flight are completed; a post-chaise is procured for him, while he sleeps, by a lady of easy virtue; he anticipates fifty difficulties: every obstacle is divinely eliminated.

And Benjamin, aware with customary self-knowledge of every working of his mind, makes the penetrating reflection that dramatic and sudden actions are no index of decision of character: on the contrary, the absence of any capacity for decision, and the corresponding sensation that nothing you do is really done, lands you neatly in the decisive fact on which at no moment can you be said to have decided. . . .

The sun is up. Down the grey streets a few early carts are rumbling to market. They pass the closed windows behind which Monsieur Benay, full-fed, lies uneasily dreaming; on, over the cobbles, past the house where Madame de Charrière has just closed the shutters and settled herself off with a dose of opium.

But Benjamin is speeding on the Calais road, his mind in a starry whirl. He thinks of Mademoiselle Pourrat's demure face of wonder, of the lovely lady who got him the post-chaise, of the history of polytheism, of the duty of freedom and the impossibility of free-will; behaving like a madman, reasoning like a philosopher, in flight from his debts, in flight from his father, in flight from himself.

Who could understand such a nature—such a coil?

Who but Madame de Charrière?

VII

THE POST-CHAISE FLEW LIKE THE WIND. WAS
not all Benjamin's life, always, alternately stag-
nant and headlong, comet-like, enveloped in
speed? At Calais a Channel packet was on the point
of putting out. On the day after his flight from Paris
the fugitive was at Dover "as if awakened from a
dream."

After despatching an apology to his father embroidered with various philosophic considerations
on the weariness of cities and the need for solitude,
Benjamin's first thoughts were for Madame de Charrière. "Little did I guess," he wrote, "while, any day
last week, I drank tea with you and talked sense, that
I would employ all my sense to commit a prodigious
folly. . . . Here I am at Dover, like one awakened
from a dream, with fifteen guineas, no servant, no
clothes, no introductions: such, madam, is my situation, and never in my life have I been conscious of
less anxiety. . . . Love me in spite of my follies: I am
a good devil at bottom. My excuses to Monsieur de
Charrière. Do not trouble yourself about my circumstances, which amuse me as though they concerned
not myself but another." Then, in reference to her
old friend Boswell's vanity, he added, "I laugh at my
own complications, and looking at my face in the
glass, exclaim, not 'Oh! Jemmy Boswell!' but 'Oh!
. . . Benjamin, Benjamin Constant!' My family
would scold me for omitting the *de* and the *Re-*

becque, but I would gladly sell these for threepence a piece."

Money, as usual in Benjamin's career, was now the urgent problem. He informed Madame de Charrière that he expected to find in London "a friend to whom I lent a large sum in Switzerland, and who, I hope, will perform a like service to me here." This friend, we learn from the "Cahier Rouge," was Mr. Edmund Lascelles. Mr. Lascelles received Benjamin very politely, but it seemed he entertained no recollection of their former ties: moreover, he regretted it, but in the absence of his banker he found himself, positively, unable to lay his hands upon a penny . . . and, with that, Mr. Edmund Lascelles became absorbed in his daily occupation, which was to sit for hours, mirror in hand, superintending the proper disposition of every individual hair on his head. His Swiss valet, it is true, was all bows to a Constant de Rebecque, and, more generous than his master, wrote proffering the sum of forty guineas. The letter, of course, miscarried: financial advantages in Benjamin's life never found the right address. No matter: he expended several of his few remaining coins on the purchase of two dogs and a monkey; quarrelled with the monkey; exchanged it for a third dog; and sold back the two others for a quarter of their price. The third beast was to pant behind Benjamin over the major part of Great Britain, till, on the last day, it sank from exhaustion on the Dover road.

Benjamin, waif in body as in spirit, wandered England, as he strayed in life, casually, to all points of the compass as chance encounters, sudden disgusts, or the prick of penury might dictate. We find him journeying to Brighthelmstone "in company with a turtle on its way to be eaten by the Prince of Wales," putting up at Wisbech to witness a wretched troupe of strolling players, riding fifty miles a day, quarrelling with innkeepers, lost in storms, and at last, penniless, making a dash for Edinburgh, and spending a fortnight of continuous carnival with his old student friends, almost as needy as himself. "At twenty nothing seemed more natural than to say to my friends 'I have come three hundred leagues to take supper with you; I haven't a penny; entertain me; make much of me; drink with me; thank me; and lend me money for my return.' I was convinced this language must charm them." And it did. He was "received with transports of joy, since the singularity of the expedition was the kind of thing that the English appreciate."

And not the English alone. Madame de Charrière, away in Paris, playing through her slow minuet with Tomeoni, became absent-minded over the harpsichord. The movement of Benjamin's figure in her brain would never keep time to stately music. She had always responded tenderly to the absurd. "Ah! James Boswell!"—he had been laughable too; yes, but "Ah! . . . Benjamin, Benjamin Constant!" So Zélide returned to Colombier; and Zélide laughed; for beside her complacently in the heavy carriage sat Monsieur de Charrière, but in her mind moved a vagabond image, the image of a young man on "an extremely small white horse, hideously ugly, and very old."

And Benjamin had an eye for background, too. He described himself to her in all the bewildering variety of his moods, in settings that made them exquisitely vivid. A vagabond image—a spirit perpetually questioning the borders between life and death: who could fail to be touched by the picture of such a wanderer in the storm, when, near Brandon, "a frightful tempest overtook me: I lost my way in the wind, the rain, and the hail; not a tree, a house, or a bush; after wandering an hour in the mist, I found myself under a gibbet where two wretched corpses had been hanging for a few hours or days, their feet all but touching my head, and their bodies, motioned by the wind, making a kind of melancholy whistle in the air"?

That was one Benjamin—the haunted, solitary pessimist who was to write "Adolphe." But for the most part, with an irony which he instinctively assumed to cover and protect his lonely intensity of life, he preferred to paint himself for her eyes, as he did for his own, in a grotesque light. "I would give— no, not money—but a smile of Mademoiselle Pourrat, to be well rid of my accursed spectacles. They give me an odd appearance, and the astonishment they create destroys the possibility of immediate intimacy—the only kind of intimacy I desire. People are so occupied with staring at me that they forget to answer. . . . My spectacles and my clothes, which are much too gentleman-like, give me the air of a *broken* gentleman: nothing could be more inconvenient. For common people like their equals; they hate poverty, and they hate rank; and so a poor-looking gentleman is doubly insulted and avoided. My one hope is to be taken for a commercial traveller." . . .

No; take him rather, this lanky figure on a low, scraggy horse, for lean Don Quixote, ceaselessly tilting at windmills of his mind.

"You have in my letters a true image of my mind: you see how everything alternates, meets, and mingles in my unhappy head—high and low, gay and sad, despair and folly." He covered the canvas for her with its high and low lights, splashes of sudden colour, and dark hopeless patches flecked with irony. He told her how on Windermere, black and wrinkled with storm, he had been powerfully overtaken by that recurrent impulse of suicide: "but there were two sailors who would have fished me up, and I do not wish to drown, as I poisoned myself, all for nothing." . . . But the sun shone out, and he travelled on through Westmoreland—"through the beautiful part, for one part is horrible, resembling Switzerland"—lyrically happy once more, exulting in England, with its beauty, its orderly little towns, its good-natured uninterfering people, and the absence of police "who make the guilty their pretext and the innocent their prey." He had six louis; he had (what we unhappily have not) all Madame de Charrière's letters; he had his horse and his dog; and if need be he would sell his watch, and travel like Goldsmith with a barrel-organ, on foot, across France, through Switzerland, and end up—at Colombier.

Colombier, the one refuge; Our Lady of Colombier, to whom else should a pilgrim offer his vows? Madame de Charrière had become the fixed centre of Benjamin's nomad imagination.

He wrote letters to her from wayside inns, he wrote letters from the back of his bony white horse, a letter of fifteen folio sheets, freakish letters from you never knew where: "Letters from Patterdale, addressed to Madame C. de Z."—they would make a book; long psychological narratives, all about himself. They were the exact counterpart of those interminable pages Zélide had written at night from the castle of Zuylen, twenty years before, to his uncle. But now Zélide was ready to play audience, to sit back, and watch and applaud, satisfied, as Hermenches had been, to be the spectator—the chosen spectator—of a younger life.

It was as if she heard her own voice speaking. "One of your happy qualities," he wrote, "is to understand everything however one may express it."

And again, "I guarantee the truth of half I write to you, which I have no patience to re-read. Read me, decide for yourself, and believe me as much as you can. Offer your unbelief to God! Your incredulity is worth a thousand times the credulity of another."

So, between grave and gay, Benjamin's Odyssey in England drew to a close. It ended, as was right, on the note of comedy. For some time he stayed with Mr. Bridges, the excellent evangelical vicar of Wadanhoe, "in return for whose manifold kindness," write Benjamin, "I willingly lent myself to religious practices sufficiently different from my own." For Mr. Bridges for an hour every evening "literally rolled upon the ground," beating his forehead on the planks, and vigorously smiting himself in the presence of his kneeling servants, and was thrown into veritable despair by the slightest interruption of these exercises. And, last of all, Benjamin sought out his friend Kentish, who indeed had lavishly offered every verbal assistance, but was at pains to give his hospitality a wounding character far more insupportable than the pious demands of the vicar. Kentish invited Benjamin to his board rather as a pauper to be fed than a friend to be welcomed, and apologized daily for the obvious scarcity of the fare, observing that it was calculated for two persons, himself and his wife. Benjamin left the house in disgust. He decided suddenly to rejoin his father, who had written in a truly heartbreaking strain imploring his immediate return. He mounted; he rode at a gallop down the Dover road. The faithful cur who had followed his travels fell exhausted by the wayside; and Benjamin sent it to Kentish with a politely expressed hope that, as he could treat a friend like a dog, he would not fail to treat this dog like a friend. Years afterwards, it is recorded, Kentish displayed this animal sentimentally to a cousin of Benjamin's as a pledge of intimate friendship, a tribute of gratitude, and a memento of happy days. . . .

But Benjamin's mind, despite his pleasantry, was overcast. The figure of his father rose dark across the Channel, formidable, resentful, anxiously pathetic. There would be a terrible meeting, reproaches, threats. . . . And, after, beyond that, the smile, the appreciation, the soothing wit of Madame de Charrière, the exquisite understanding of the only person in the world who understood. But between them loomed the colonel. Benjamin did not doubt the truth and shy profundity of Juste's affection. He loved his father no less sensitively than he feared him, and his affection was deepened by the consciousness of the pain he had caused. That last letter had tortured him with remorse; Juste had written convincingly that he was ill with grief, that Benjamin if he stayed longer would be responsible for his death. Benjamin hastened on his way, wrestling with his own timidity, nerving himself for the encounter. He would take his castigation in good part, and then—at last—he would speak frankly, thrusting aside the screen of difficult reserve. He longed to explain himself, to ask his father's pardon, to gain his confidence.

He arrived at Bois-le-Duc unannounced. The colonel was at whist with three officers of his regiment.

"Is that you?" he asked, over his shoulder. "You must be tired. Go to bed."

The three officers rose, saluted, and left father and son alone. Benjamin turned timidly to obey the injunction.

"Your coat is torn," observed Colonel Juste de Constant. "That," he added, "is what I always feared about your expedition."

And on this they separated. The subject was not reopened. Three days later the frozen silence was still unbroken.

Benjamin left for Switzerland.

He arrived at Colombier, on foot, "at eight o'clock on the evening of 3rd October 1787." In the "Journal Intime" he records, religiously, the anniversary of this date.

And "Madame de Charrière received me with raptures of delight."

VIII

THE AUTUMN AND WINTER OF THIS YEAR
were to remain in the memories of Zélide and
Benjamin as an oasis in the stony waste of their
two lives. Other pools and palms Benjamin was destined to pursue; but, most often, when he reached
them they were mirage, or shelters more stormy than
the storm. And, for Zélide, fate reserved dust, foun-
tainless dust.

The first meeting at Colombier was brimmed with
gaiety, and brief. There were, first, Madame de Charrière's "raptures of joy," and after that she had to listen, with what composure she could, to the poignant
story of Juste de Constant and the torn coat, and then
to laugh, with that toss back of her head, at a whole
gallery of English portraits. She knew England and
could appreciate their truth. She could catch the very
sniff of Edmund Lascelles, with his elegant smatter-
ing of Horace, his valet, and his hours in front of the
pier glass; she could hear the rustle of old Lady Charlotte Wentworth, Lord Rockingham's sister, the great
Whig lady whom Benjamin had contemplated with
peculiar veneration; she could feel the thrill of good
Mr. Bridges' forehead beaten fervently upon the
floor, and with all her heart she echoed Benjamin's
enthusiasm for a country where, more than anywhere
in the world, the individual is respected and the eccentric indulged. Monsieur de Salgas had been
wholly wrong in saying she was born for Paris. For

to England, the home of exaggerated personalities, of freedom to do and think as you please, Zélide, like Benjamin, belonged.

But if Benjamin's spiritual home was England, his household gods were nearer by, at Lausanne; and by the commands of the colonel he had to repair immediately to Beausoleil, to be placed under the close surveillance of uncle, aunt, and the whole clan of Constant cousins. He did not, however, lose touch with his friend at Colombier; letters were interchanged once or even twice a day, poems, fragments for the libretto of the opera on which she was now eagerly engaged. His father wrote that he had procured him the post of Chamberlain at the Court of Brunswick; but Benjamin was now too ill to start on another journey. He lived a life apart, in the care of doctors, resting after the racket of his exploits in Paris and England; Don Quixote is tired of tilting; Don Juan is indisposed.

When at last he was able to move, he set out not, as the colonel demanded, for Brunswick, but once more for Colombier. And, as always, Benjamin arrived with a twinkle in his eye and a characteristic story for Zélide. For, on the way, as the result of some gallantries exchanged between his dog and that of a passing sportsman, he had involved himself in a quarrel which had led to a challenge followed in due course by a duel in grand style. Benjamin, whose indifference to life amounted to a secret predilection for death, had been throughout in the highest spirits; his gaiety, even more than his courage, had quenched the bravado of his adversary. The families of both combatants had precipitated themselves along the Neuchâtel road at the news of the encounter, which seems to have terminated to Benjamin's credit, after wavering, characteristically, between tragedy and farce. The diary of one of his cousins confirms the tale.

In spite of this adventure, which must have re-called to Madame de Charrière the histrionic Ben-jamin of Paris days, she found him changed. The har-lequin had turned gentle and domestic. The hectic excitement engendered in him by Parisian life had been dissipated in those solitary spaces he had tra-versed on his little white horse; England, where no one indulged his passion for abstract argument, had lowered the pressure of his intellectual agitation; fa-tigue and illness had done the rest. He was looking for repose; and he found at Colombier the easy re-laxation of home life, which home does not always supply. The freezing irony of Colonel Juste de Con-stant had been the best preparation for the amenities of Colombier. Benjamin—"the wounded pigeon"—had come to roost in the Charrière dovecot.

She, too, in her Dutch cap, surrounded by a maze of manuscripts, of proof sheets, and pencilled op-eras, was more homely than at Paris. Her time was gaily filled with these occupations; the black gloom that Pastor Chaillet had found so romantic and so ungodly had been dispelled by Benjamin. He had richly occupied her thoughts, and now that he was come he slipped gently and naturally into the routine of her days. Of a morning he would sit by her crimson bed, laughing with her over the small human comedy of the house, dissecting Mademoiselle Moula's affected modesty, dealing very gently with Monsieur de Charrière, but very strictly with Mademoiselle Henriette. And soon they would be sitting opposite each other on either side of a black table littered with papers, Madame de Charrière retouching a scene from her "lyrical tragedy in imitation of Euripides" or adding a page to her "Political Observations and Conjectures," and Benjamin making notes for the history of polytheism upon the backs of playing cards. Now and again he would snatch a page from her to correct her semicolons, or, rising and looking over her shoulder, would read out, sonorously, some line of blank verse that had slipped into her prose. But he never showed her what he had written on his pack of cards. In the projects that really interested his ambition, Benjamin wanted encouragement and praise: the cold douche of criticism he could easily administer for himself; the history of polytheism was not for her eyes. Oftenest Madame de Charrière would be beside her harpsichord. She sat over it, fingering out the airs of her opera, while her hair was being dressed; she returned to it at all hours. Her persistence at that instrument was Benjamin's sole distress. A crimson bed, a bath sometimes, a harpsichord always: everything was collected in that small chamber away upstairs; two tables, piled with papers that no one might touch; books, now seldom read; a *chaise longue* for Benjamin's lanky legs, and in a corner the fireplace she had put in after her marriage—you may see it there with the date, and see, if you will, the ghosts of Benjamin and Zélide crouched over their tisane. Infinite talk: if Madame de Charrière's wit flagged for an instant Benjamin would give it a flick with his *"Eh bien, Madame?"* and wait for the next move. A mingling of wit and of intimacy; a perfect freedom, a ceaseless range of ideas; and, between two solitary and complicated natures, an absolute understanding: each knew the rareness of what was taking place. Towards dawn Benjamin would clamber down the winding secret stair that led to a small room with a cracked ceiling—his lair on the landing below. Even then a sudden idea, an epigram on the night's conversation, a couplet, a parody, a polished gallantry disguising its tenderness—any of these would furnish the excuse for a note at early morning from one bedroom to the other, received and answered with readiness and delight. So without interruption the intimacy grew, and the day mixed with night; the hours went their round. And sometimes when the fire was steady or a single candle burned between them, he would watch the dark silhouette of her profile on the wall, and note the elusive beauty that even her shadow possessed.

These things would be remembered; recalled with the enchantment that belongs to trifles; vainly driven out from the mind at last in the desolation of estrangement; pictures in the memory, trifling, ineffaceable scenes.

There is a delicate affection in the exactitude with which Benjamin will evoke such images in his letters. "It is ten minutes past ten," he will write, "and, on such a day, we were sitting in the kitchen by the fire, and from behind us the maid would get up from time to time to feed the fire with little sticks of wood which she sat breaking to the right length, and we were talking of the affinity between genius and madness. We were happy; at least I was. There is a cruel pleasure in foreseeing the moment of a separation which will hurt. It gives a value to every instant."

It is the tone of the recollection which is here significant rather than the facts recalled. And yet the image is vivid, too. A curious setting, the kitchen of Colombier, for those two figures. Sainte Beuve has said that Benjamin Constant had greater brilliance than anyone of his epoch with the single exception of Voltaire; and Benjamin, on his side, has repeatedly affirmed that no woman had the intelligence of Madame de Charrière, original without paradox, perpetually surprising and yet scrupulously just. Longhi should have painted them: a piece of eighteenth-century *genre*; and in the shadows of the kitchen he might have placed those dumb, surprised onlookers, Monsieur de Charrière and his sisters, or Pastor Chaillet looming in the door. As it is, there is little trace remaining of their irony or their tenderness, such slender record does happiness leave. Nothing is left for our eyes but a black silhouette, cut by the scissors of demure Mademoiselle Moula, of Benjamin, with his finger on his lips. . . .

But if the wit of Benjamin had an affinity with that of Voltaire, his humanity was entirely different, more spontaneous, warmer, more lovable in its weakness, more modern, altogether, in its perplexity. The Voltairean period, the sharply intellectual stage, of the friendship between Benjamin and Zélide had been run through in Paris. The second stage, at Colombier, is radically different. It is now a question of a simpler, more profoundly human affinity. A stronger emotion has entered; has stood the test of their hardness, their irony, and their scepticism. And, if it has still something ascetic in its style, its hold on their imagination is all the greater.

They are inveterate talkers still, but now there are quieter currents beneath that rapid-moving surface. He who was to write "Adolphe" had no need for many words, nor could he mistake for hardness the reserve of her who had written "Caliste."

For a short while they were parted. Benjamin

moved to Neuchâtel to complete the cure of his malady in the hands of his doctor. A flood of letters filled this brief interval; messengers went to and fro carrying books lent by the polite and self-effacing Monsieur de Charrière, or manuscripts sent by Zélide for Benjamin to revise. It was a mark of singular submission on her part, for she piqued herself on her classic French. *"Ainsi qu'ordonnez, ferai, noble dame,"* he replied with elaborate pedantry, *"votre feuille reviserai, et corrigerai ce qu'ignorance ou légèreté auront commis. Ensuite la dite feuille ferai partir pour immortalité et admiration."* It was still on some such note of mockery that they most often wrote.

But once again Colonel Juste is thundering in the distance. Rumours of his son's intimacy with Madame de Charrière, that dangerous woman, have reached him from Lausanne. Well or ill, Benjamin must leave forthwith for Brunswick. "My family," observed Benjamin bitterly, "are more concerned for my chastity than for my life."

He set out for Brunswick, in mid-winter; riding the dark roads with his mind full of resentment at the ceaseless interference of his family, their failure to understand that in Madame de Charrière he had found, not a mistress, but a friend who offered precisely the penetrating and protective affection which they had never given him. And again, as in his escape to England, he wrote her at every stage of the journey a full history of his thoughts. But now his letters are no longer the artificial and sometimes mocking *boutades* with which he had, till now, played up to her ironic appreciation of his peculiarity. They have a note of definite sincerity, a new note of fervour. "The roads are terrible, the wind bitter, and I am sad, sadder to-day than yesterday, as yesterday I was sadder than the day before, and to-morrow shall be sadder than I am to-day. It is difficult and painful to leave you for a day, and every day adds its pain to that of the day before. . . . So long as you live, and I live, I shall say to myself, in no matter what trouble, 'there is Colombier in the world.' Before I knew you I used to say, 'if they torment me too much I can kill myself,' but now, 'if they make my life unendurable, I have my retreat.' . . . I owe you certainly my health, and probably my life: I owe you much more, since this life, in spite of all Pastor Chaillet may say to the contrary, is an unhappy business, and you have made it a happy one. . . . I would give ten years of health at Brunswick for a year's illness at Colombier. . . . You are my harbour; and if it needs a storm for me to be allowed it, then let the storm come and shatter all my masts and tear all my sails. . . . *Adieu, mille fois bonne, mille fois chère, mille fois aimée.*" The old parade of irony is completely dropped; and when Constant, the master of phrases, used the simple, the universal, language, Madame de Charrière knew that the words meant more than they would from another.

She knew, too, the significance of his way of dwelling on every detail of their companionship, his reluctance to break the thread, his human attempt to realize, hour by hour, what was happening in the life he had left. "What are you doing, madam, at this moment? It is a quarter past six. . . . You are coming down the spiral stair, and you give a glance into my room. I am a little in your thoughts."

Learned writers have discussed, but have not satisfactorily resolved the question—were Madame de Charrière and Benjamin lovers? The subject has its pedantries like any other. I will not explore them. Psychologically, the character of their relation is abundantly clear; technically, the inquiry would be inconclusive.

What is clear, and the sequel will show it still more clearly, is that this man and this woman, widely separated in age, obsessed each other. The attraction was between two minds, bewilderingly akin. To each the self-conscious analysis of every pulse and instant of life, of every problem and situation, was as necessary as a vice. Benjamin was a libertine when the mood was on him, just as in other moods he became an ambitious author or a politician; but he was a thinker always; and his intellect never worked with more startling clearness than when his emotions were involved. The thing he shared with Madame de Charrière—this rapid clarity and ceaseless gymnastic of the mind—was not a mood, but the man himself. Understanding that, holding him by that, she held him as strongly as any woman could. Of the three women who, he declared later, had "entirely determined" his life—Madame de Staël, Madame Recamier, and Madame de Charrière—the last, if she had not played her cards disastrously, might have enjoyed the most lasting dominion.

On Madame de Charrière's side the obsession was natural enough. Her fantastic reasoning had led her into a marriage that was no better than a void. Now, in middle age, a kind of *alter ego* had suddenly crossed her path. She found in Benjamin a blend of fantasy and logic like her own, a creature as solitary as herself and as eagerly curious for every experiment in the human chemistry, craving, as she craved, insatiably, for a shared analysis of life. She whose versatility had been unable to circumvent the blank wall of Monsieur de Charrière, suddenly found herself influencing, controlling, and—as she thought— protecting this new, mobile, and responsive personality. Her tyrant benevolence found its natural victim in his comic helplessness, her subtlety its keenest exercise in tracing the elusive doubleness of his mind and action. He was complicated, generous, picturesque, unhappy. That she should love him, and in due course lose him—a man half her age—is natural enough: it is classic.

On his side the force of the obsession is less normal; but then Constant was everything except normal; and his abnormality, in which he delighted, implied a profound loneliness, from which he despaired; she alone had entry to the lonely centre of the maze. By her quick understanding of him she had made herself the one fixed firm point in the *tour de force* of his life. She knew him—unpredictable, yet instinctively and almost childishly loyal; sophisticated, and yet wholly impulsive; frivolous, only to hide how deeply his seriousness was always baffled and perplexed. He might wear mask upon mask: she would not quarrel with it; she knew that the mask was as essential to him as what lay behind: neither more nor less. No other woman had done that. No other woman would have the brains to do it. Her hold on him was so great that she over-reached herself. She analysed. She explored. She guided. One thing she did not understand in time: that Benjamin might weary of being understood.

For that craving to be understood is a craving of adolescence. He seemed the eternal adolescent; his mind had never been young; it seemed that neither would it ever grow up. But Benjamin's reason is more flexible than hers. It will learn from life that vitality is the supreme argument, before which the reason may reasonably remain mute. And Madame de Staël, vulgar perhaps but vital, Madame de Staël, at whose mind he and Madame de Charrière had mocked, will sweep him, radiantly consenting, in her train.

But not yet.

IX

WHATEVER COLONEL JUSTE DE CONSTANT contrived for his son's welfare was always of a comic unsuitability. At six he had delivered him into the charge of a profligate tutor. At thirteen he had sought to place him at the University of Oxford. At nineteen he had left him to run wild in Paris. And now, at twenty, he conceived that Benjamin would find profit and happiness with a gold-braided coat, a sword, and a wand as gentleman usher in a German court; Benjamin, of the ungainly figure, was to walk backwards, and to have for his sole function in life the performance of ceremonial bows. Benjamin, of the restless spirit, was to spend his evenings nodding assent to the platitudes of fatuous *Hofdamen*. The ardent democrat was to be a *Kammerjunker*. The finest wit of his generation was to be exercised in a circle of princes who neared, or overstepped, the borders of certified imbecility.

What matter (declared the Constant family in conclave) so long as Benjamin was torn from the bonds of Madame de Charrière?

The Duke of Brunswick, nephew of Frederick the Great, was a formidable and serious autocrat, a just administrator, a fine soldier, a polished and upright martinet. He nourished a profound contempt for his courtiers, and preferred the most insignificant of his soldiers to the first of his chamberlains. Benjamin, in his presence, was a frozen icicle of respect. The

139

Duchess, sister of King George III, did not disguise her malicious anticipation that young Constant in the discharge of his courtly duty would be a spectacle worth seeing. (And what the devil is there so funny about it? muttered Benjamin.) Besides these, there was the Princess Caroline (our Queen Caroline), a hunchback prince, and a host of obese royalties revolving in three planetary systems, for in addition to the Duke's court there were the courts of the Dowager and Hereditary Duchesses. As for the Crown Prince, stout, greasy and short-sighted (he had been known to bow ceremoniously to a circle of empty chairs) he, according to one observer, was "only less idiotic than his brother who was an idiot completely."

To these stellar worlds was Benjamin removed from the kitchen of Colombier.

It was like a bad dream. He wandered in solitude round the mediaeval ramparts of Brunswick, and thought of Madame de Charrière. He lost his way in the dim and slushy streets, his mind astray in the scenes he had left. In the ballrooms of the palace he stood absent and constrained. Across the distance that separated them her image seemed more substantial, her ghost more companionable, than these Germans physically present with their thick speech, their ponderous mirth and puffy etiquette. Every afternoon a very stiff and very tall chamberlain came to fetch him, and conducted him in dead silence to pay his ceremonial visits. On foot over the snow, down the Gothic streets, the two lean figures in court dress might be seen, shivering and slipping at every step, side by side, without a word. Only on the doorstep of his lodgings, "*J'aurai l'honneur de fenir vous prendre*," the German would pronounce, breaking the stillness at last, "*temain à quatre heures et temie.*"

At court Benjamin remained silent and aloof. In vain Madame de Charrière entreated him to reveal himself, and win the credit which his flashing intelligence deserved. He preferred to remain a dark lantern. He had matched his wits with Madame de Charrière who "had enough wit to make Germany tremble"; what did it matter to him whether Brunswick decided "*qu'il afoit beaucoup de l'esprit*" or "*qu'il afoit médiocrement de l'esprit*"? As for the manners of his fellow courtiers, he observed from his corner of the ballroom that, here, gaiety consisted in losing one's breath and politeness in losing one's balance. A disquieting figure, this tall young man with the ironical light in his greenish eyes, who never "puffed and blew" when he laughed, who seemed while you spoke to him to fall into a kind of trance, who agreed with you so gravely, and then sometimes of a sudden, in a manner all his own, was so inappropriately, indeed so quite unaccountably, gay.

Once more, as at Paris, the influence of Madame de Charrière is confirming Benjamin in his detachment from mankind. It was too late now to urge him to show his mettle. She has built for him a fortress of intimacy and understanding; within it he is at peace. But she has sharpened his irony, and created between him and the world around—that conventional, necessary world from which she herself had withdrawn—a deep and perilous gulf. So the friendly interest excited by Benjamin's arrival gave place at Brunswick to suspicion and reproach.

He has described the experience, and recognized her influence, in a passage of "Adolphe." "At court the fatigue of so much purposeless excitement led me to prefer solitude to the insipid pleasures I was called upon to share. I hated no one; but scarcely anyone inspired interest in me; and men are wounded by indifference: they attribute it to ill-will or affectation, since they are unwilling to believe that boredom in their company is a merely natural experience. . . . If, at other times, weary of my own silence, I gave rein to any pleasantries, the spirit of mockery, once aroused, led me beyond all bounds, and I disclosed in one day the follies I had remarked for a month. The confidants of my sudden and involuntary outpourings did not thank me for them; and they were in the right. For it was the need of speech that had seized me, and not the desire to confide. I had formed during my conversations with the woman who first developed my ideas an insuperable dislike to all commonplace maxims and dogmas. When, therefore, I heard mediocrity holding forth with complaisance upon the principles of morality, use and religion (matters which men like to put on the same level) I felt myself pricked to contradiction; not because I would have adopted opposite principles, but because I was impatient of so firm and heavy a conviction. I scarcely know indeed what instinct it was that warned me to distrust these generalities, so free from all restriction, so devoid of all half-lights. Fools make their system of morals into a compact and indivisible mass in order to leave their actions free in all details. Through this conduct I very soon earned for myself a great reputation for frivolity and malice. . . . Those whom I had carelessly laughed at found it convenient to make common cause with the principles they accused me of questioning. . . . One might have thought that in drawing attention to their absurdity I had betrayed some confidence they had imposed; or that by showing themselves to me such as they were, they had obtained from me a vow of discretion. I was not conscious of having signed so onerous a bond. They had found pleasure in letting themselves go; I, in observing and describing them; that which they called a perfidy seemed to me an innocent and legitimate indulgence.

"I am not intending to justify myself here; I have long ago renounced this facile and perilous employment of an inexperienced mind, I only wish to say (and that more for others than for myself who am now protected from the world) that time is needed to accustom oneself to the human race, such as self-interest, affectation, vanity, and fear have made it. The astonishment of youth at the aspect of a society so false and so unnatural, betrays a simple heart rather than a malicious spirit. Besides, society has nothing to fear. She weighs so much upon us all, her heavy influence is so powerful, that she takes but little time in fashioning us in the universal mould. We are then astonished only at our old surprise, and are very comfortable in our new shape; just as we end by breathing freely in a crowded playhouse, where, on first entering, we could hardly breathe at all."

These reflections reveal the impersonal wisdom that underlay the surface of Benjamin's passions and agitated moods, a solitary wisdom akin to Madame de Charrière's own, but more serenely humorous, and truer. For in the last resort he was ready to take his part in the play with a good grace. "And all the men and women merely players": yes, all: he too, among them, fashioned at last to the same mould; so, more and more, he saw himself. But Madame de Charrière stood like a frozen player: she surveyed the strutting scene, and forgot that life is a theatre built without an auditorium.

Safe in his Brunswick lodgings, Benjamin plunged himself in studies of Greek history, translated German, and accumulated notes for that history of Religion which made the one persistent thread in his life. Forty-three years later, on the day of his death, he corrected the proofs of the last volume. Neither the human passion nor the politics which came to divide his career, nor yet the alternation of enthusiasms and despairs which never ceased to sway his monetary and unstable nature, could wholly defeat in Benjamin the scholar's patience or turn him from that lonely adventure of the mind. Already he was feeling his way to an anthropological study of religion that was to range beyond the tidy universe of Voltaire. Madame de Charrière could not follow him here. Yet he found his standard of expression fixed by her own language—those minted thoughts that had so lucid a value and so honest a ring. In all he now wrote he sought to satisfy her test. "How much I gain," he told her, "in making you my audience. You render my ideas clearer, you lighten my labour, you simplify my style." And he dedicated some historical essays at this period "to her who created Caliste and resembles her; to her who may be wrongly known, but, once known can never be forgotten . . . the most brilliant and yet the simplest and most feeling of women, the tenderest and truest friend."

In these days he took little part in the pleasures of the court, and sought out the society of scholars— "more for the sake of their libraries than of their conversation." The opera afforded little temptation; one of the actresses had a wooden leg and a single eye. He sought, under Madame de Charrière's influence, to break himself of his most powerful vice: on the

145

back of a knave of hearts he wrote out a mighty oath to abjure gambling, and sent it to Colombier. From the tedium of Brunswick, study was one constant refuge; the other was to unburden himself of his thoughts and schemes and ironies in letters to Zélide. He returned to these letters every few hours; longer and longer they grew; the couriers left Brunswick, but the interminable manuscript remained on Constant's desk, unposted. In one drawer he laid the notes for the history of polytheism, another was set apart for letters from Colombier. But why did they not come? He waited for that firm script sealed with the head of Perseus. But *petit Persée* tarried; what is passing in Zélide's mind?

Assuredly Zélide had every reason to be satisfied with her ascendancy. In the midst of the phantom court Benjamin moved as in a trance. In a veritable trance; for sometimes—so completely did Madame de Charrière absorb the underworld of his consciousness—she seemed actually to have been present in the gilded rooms. "To-night, playing loto, I was thinking of you as you may readily believe. So vividly was the idea of you interpenetrated with the place, that, as I undressed, 'Who was it," I kept asking myself, 'that I found so entrancing at the Duchess's?' and then realized that it had been you, you at two hundred and fifty leagues distance." And again, "Playing cards to-night with one of the princes, I came to forget you were not at Brunswick, 'I shall be seeing her,' I said; and so strong was the idea that I peacefully endured the boredom of the game and of the supper, waiting for the moment when I should rejoin this vague yet vividly desired person. Then suddenly I realized that the friend who was to console me this very evening was none other than yourself. I had the utmost difficulty in grasping the idea of our separation." In one of his reveries he planned to elope with Madame de Charrière to Paris. "Her husband's temperament is such as to free her from any obligation: he takes little part in her successes, none in her pleasures; his sister keeps the house. We could be happy together in Paris, in London, anywhere, come what might. Life is short; why hesitate?"

Stiff duke, hunchback and half-witted prince, blowsy *Hofdamen*, tinselled courtiers, all were unreal. The rococo mirrors curling on the damask walls reflected the figures of a dream. Zélide alone in his life is trenchant, limpid, actual. In the midst of phantoms, she is there.

Zélide at last has found a human being in her own likeness; she has touched in Benjamin a perfect probity of intelligence, responsive to her own; in that ceaseless dialogue of his thoughts she takes her part; she has dominated him, she surrounds him, a second self; she is the benignant atmosphere through which he moves. At last she has created something according to the pattern of her mind.

X

AND ALREADY, AWAY THERE AT COLOMBIER, she is at work destroying it.

Already her sceptical reason is busy, undermining her happiness, gnawing at her hopes.

So long as Benjamin had been merely a picturesque novelty, a streak of colour suddenly crossing the drab texture of her life, she had surrendered herself entirely to the enjoyment of him. Now that she loved him her reason arose, challenged, and stood guard. Understanding too well the mobility of Benjamin's nature and his lively susceptibility to every experience, she took it for granted that new impressions must soon efface the impression she had made. Soon; already? She wrote to him: "In some weeks, in a few days perhaps, you will have new habits and occupations. Oh, then I will not write to you so often, for the lively pleasures of your way of life will take the place of my friendship." He replies, "Barbet, Barbet" (it was one of his nicknames for her), "you are very lovable, and I love you tenderly, but your reasoning is very bad. Singular and charming person, tell me, where is this modesty leading? Do you really suppose that after three or four weeks I shall have formed the habit of some German fräulein or hofdame who will take your place? That your gentleness, goodness, and charm are something easily replaced, easily forgotten? . . . That, even if I were so hard as to think without tenderness of the sympathy which united us, I could be so stupid as not to miss that mutual intuition of thought which passed perpetually from me to you and from you to me? Nothing will make me forget my happiness with you; no habits I shall ever form will make you less dear to me; nothing will take your place. I say this for the last time, for it hurts me that I should have to justify myself. It is a great gladness to me to write that I love you; but it is an even greater pain that you should doubt it. Henceforward I shall regard every page in which you abandon yourself to these doubts as so much blank paper. I shall say: 'Madame de Charrière has just sufficient affection to wish me to know that she has not wholly forgotten me, and, to this end, she has neatly folded a sheet of white paper and sealed it with little Perseus: I am grateful to her: I regret that she should have found nothing to say on her blank sheet.' . . . Good-night, I love you as much as ever any man has loved, or has loved you. I wish I could see you stretching out your hand to me from your crimson bed. I wish I had turned back to see you once again before I left. . . . May you be very, very, very happy."

But she persisted in her distrust. She would not cheat herself again. What of the tears shed over Ca-liste? She had lost her lover at Geneva; and how should she now, an ageing woman, hold this will o' the wisp of a Benjamin? The very headiness and swiftness with which he had abandoned himself to her influence, what were these but a proof that a new influence would soon take its place? And why, after all, had his capture been complete? Mademoiselle Louise, over her knitting, had observed that Monsieur Constant's illness was so lucky: "You could never have been on the terms you were, here, with Monsieur Constant, but for his malady. Had it not been for that, he would have been very quickly bored: he would have gone every day to Neuchâtel. . . ." Now if only Mademoiselle Henriette had said that! But on Mademoiselle Louise's lips the words were a benevolent warning; and were they not true?

"I say, with humility, the words are true," wrote Zélide to Benjamin. "And had I said to you—had I dared say—'you must not settle far from me and leave me out of your life, for I am necessary to you,' what outcries would have been raised at my presumption, my folly, at my selfishness above all. . . . The world will not allow one to think one may be necessary, or sufficient to a single fellow being. It is always careful to forestall or destroy this happy and innocent illusion."

The world of Lausanne, in particular, took care to effect this by bringing to Madame de Charrière's notice every possible insinuation against Benjamin's loyalty. Facts—were they facts?—that contradicted his assertions. Things done, or said—but were they really said?—and twisted by gossip, torturer of

pride. Phrases he had used—she would not listen to
them, she would not put them on paper; phrases that
could not possibly be admitted, that seemed to bear
the authentic stamp; phrases that must have been his,
facts that must, yet could not be facts. Fictions . . .
echoes of facts?

Benjamin was such a talker—the context would
be everything. No, Benjamin was so inconstant—
and anything might be true. . . .

So Madame de Charrière stirred the cauldron of
her pessimism, her diffidence, her humility, and her
doubt, and into the dark potion she dropped the
small poisons of suspicion.

And Benjamin at Brunswick sat over his unposted
protestations of devotion, and built his hopes on the
understanding of the one human being who understood him too well. "If a letter came from you to
break this eternity of silence!" he called; and then
"little Perseus" arrived, and plunged Benjamin in
dismay.

He broke out: "I have often noticed in you that
melancholy and humble diffidence, but please remember that it ruins all the joy of our friendship. . . .
How can you think that I shall ever not set a price—
a great, an infinite price—upon it? You are as cruel
as you are unreasonable; and if you persist in this diffidence, which I frankly call more insulting than
'humble,' your friendship, which I would not renounce for all the happiness of life, will become to

both of us a source of sorrow. In God's name enough of these reserves. If they are genuine they are harsh and mortifying to me; if they are a literary ornament is it not cruel to exercise your brilliance, two hundred and fifty leagues away, at the cost of my misery? . . . I shall take you as meaning, 'I have no confidence whatever in you, and I regard my interest in you as a weakness; I have not sufficient respect for you to say frankly: my doubts are these, or these, explain them if you can?' . . . I implore you to make no mysteries. I will admit to whatever is justified, and will not weary you with long replies to whatever is false. I shall say: 'You are mistaken': I venture to hope you will believe me. Only let your next letter make clear what is in your mind."

In vain Benjamin entreated and cajoled. Madame de Charrière would not explain herself. Long ago she had spent years in courting and pursuing Bellegarde whom she did not love; now she loved Benjamin, and all her effort seemed to be to exasperate him by her doubts and estrange him by her hardness. Her reason had justified her plan to marry Bellegarde: it turned devil's advocate against her vital impulse to hold Benjamin. Secretly, within herself, she believed that she could not hold a man so much younger than herself. Firmly she hid her unhappiness beneath a tone of light good-humoured refusal to take the situation seriously.

"I have lost everything, and you make a joke of it,"

protested Benjamin. "You are determined always to doubt me: the wise course would be to abandon our letters completely. The idea is terrible to me: I have not the strength; I must bear with you, and write. But you must expect no more gaiety from me, no more of the letters which amuse you. You have poisoned the source of what gaiety I had left. I can keep it up no more. One must love you for your goodness, because you are lovable, but that affection, thanks to the disbelief which you write of so lightheartedly is become the bitterness of sentiments, and I am in despair."

It was characteristic of Benjamin and Zélide alike to anticipate experience. Like all swiftly reasoning and introspective human beings they were quick to discover a formula for their feelings and to foresee the fatal and necessary progress of the heart. Bruised by the past, they sought to protect themselves against the future by a vivid forecast of its perils; thus they created and gave rein to their own nightmares. Like children playing at ghosts, they found themselves overtaken by the shadow of fear; and even before the spectre had taken shape they were in flight.

They were necessary one to the other. But the very qualities which, when they were together, satisfied that need, made for estrangement in the distorting medium of absence.

The castle of their hopes began visibly to totter. To this menace they reacted in precisely opposite ways.

Benjamin's cries of warning and despair might well, one would say, have reassured her fears as to his affection; but the more emotional Benjamin became, the colder and harder became Madame de Charrière. Persistently he asked for what she had given him at Colombier—the sense of a moral anchorage, which, he instinctively knew, his more passionate liaisons would never yield. Persistently she clung to what alone seemed stable and appropriate: her intellectual ascendancy. In the self-torment of her spirit this intellectual mastery took the form of pedantic rebuke.

From her childhood her heart and her intellect had been at war. Her pride and her philosophy declared that the will in that warfare must be thrown on the side of the mind. The hopes of her love for Benjamin had been built high. But something was wrong with the castle; well then, the walls must be ruthlessly subjected to the hammer and the pick, the very foundations must be dug up. Then amid the ruins, then and not before, would she consent to parley with her heart. And what was a broken heart—her own even—compared to a false syllogism? To Benjamin's touching and generous appeals she replied by pointing out, remorselessly, their slips of logic. And Benjamin's valet found his master in tears.

XI

IT MAY CONFIDENTLY BE ASSERTED THAT THE habit of letter-writing has estranged far more lovers than it has united. It is the devil's device, whereby what seems the bridge of absence becomes the very register of separation. The harmonies of life are one thing; the harmonies of literature another. A literary friendship is a very pretty art in itself; it is a singularly tricky craft if the object be to maintain the sympathies and ascendancies which have been established in the terms of physical contiguity.

To dip the quill in ink is a magical gesture: it sets free in each of us a new and sometimes a forbidding sprite, the epistolary self. The personality disengaged by the pen is something apart and often ironically diverse from that other personality of act and speech. Thus in the correspondence of lovers there will be four elements at play—four egoisms to be placated instead of two. And by this grim and mathematic law the permutations of possible offence will be calculably multiplied.

To Benjamin, while the firelight in the kitchen at Colombier played upon her features, how strong and stimulating had seemed the inexorable turn of Madame de Charrière's mind. Her hardness was something he could measure, manage, and cajole. Her eyes, with that famous half-defiant, half-caressing look they had, perpetually modified, interpreted, and humanized the sharpness of her thought. On paper, pursued to the bitter end, how ruthless those arguments became!

It took eleven days for a letter to reach Brunswick; it took over three weeks to get an answer; and yet, relentlessly, she stuck to her points and clinched her demonstrations about phrases which the emotional Benjamin, writing in agitation, had let slip a month before. She was pitiless with herself, and with her friend. "You are a kind, a good, and a very terrible lady," Monsieur de Salgas had said. Yes, terrible to others, and to herself in those moods of stoic melancholy which were the price of her proud logic.

The correspondence between them for the next few months is almost entirely lost. When we recapture the thread Benjamin is preparing Madame de Charrière to receive the news of his engagement to marry a lady of the Duchess's court, a lady nine years older than himself, Wilhelmina von Cramm.

His friend's reserves and suspicions had cast him back once more into his habitual lonely restlessness; Wilhelmina's tears (she was lonely too) had worked upon his chivalry; and, in brief, in that ghostly court of Brunswick he had found one figure of flesh and blood. And so he took his pen and wrote: "*Barbet chéri, aime-moi un peu, aime beaucoup ma Wilhelmine qui le mérite. . . . Vous l'aimez déjà, n'est-ce pas? . . . Cher bon Barbet, combien je te dois, et combien je t'aime.*"

With what expression Madame de Charrière read

this naïve appeal there is no record. It is certain that she rose, characteristically and clearly, to the large occasion. She who had strained at so many insignificant gnats, swallowed this camel, Minna, with admirable promptitude and grace.

Indeed, that was not the kind of thing she minded. For here was a plain, human appeal to generosity and good sense. She accepted it at once, and with the best possible will.

Moreover, Benjamin's decision was a source of no surprise and a few terrors for herself. Had not her intimacy with him sprung up in the very midst of his desperate courtship of Mademoiselle Pourrat? She knew Benjamin's matrimonial mind by heart. He had a fixed idea that a wife would assuage the torments of freedom. The colonel, too, was always busy with schemes of reasonable wedlock for his vagabond son, of all men the most unfitted and most eager for that state. In any case her own function as chosen confidante, chief adviser and ultimate consoler, would not be diminished. It would, most probably, be signally enlarged.

So Zélide gave Wilhelmina her blessing: and looked on. Here was Benjamin's fate. Probably his brief fate.

The future justified these intuitions.

Benjamin's addiction to matrimony was of a kind that a "Barbet" could afford to contemplate without alarm. And, years later, did he not leave his second

wife, Charlotte, hidden away for months, uncon-
fessed and unannounced, out of fear of Madame de
Staël? It was not of Benjamin's wives but of his intellectual mistresses that Madame de Charrière had
reason to be afraid.

Wilhelmina was a mistake. "*Hymen, hymen, quel
monstre!*" Madame de Charrière was to hear the cry
from Benjamin's lips before many months of marriage were out.

Meanwhile Zélide was all tact and kindness. She
received a visit from the pair at Colombier; she dis-
creetly took Minna's side in the first disputes; it is
plain that she did her best for Benjamin's happiness,
which meant that she played her own cards, in this
business, exceedingly wisely.

But there was another matter afoot; and here Madame de Charrière made a tactical error. The delays
and tribulation attending Benjamin's marriage to
Minna were only a part, and the lesser part, of what
was occupying his mind. Colonel Juste de Constant,
that tragic and saturnine figure, had irrupted once
more into the action of the drama. Or, to speak more
exactly, he had disappeared in smoke and thunder
from the stage.

The situation was this. The colonel was a shy, a noble, a lonely, a terrifying, and above all a fantastically
litigious individual. He was at this juncture engaged
in no less than thirteen simultaneous lawsuits, in ten
of which he was the plaintiff. He had made bitter

enemies among the Bernese officers of his regiment by his caustic brevity of speech; they had watched for their opportunity, and had succeeded by a malevolent intrigue in involving their chief in military disgrace. The story is a complicated one which need not here be unravelled. The Swiss National Council was markedly prejudiced; the colonel fought his suits heroically; but in a series of swift strokes the Council declared against him on almost every count, and suspended him from military duty for six months.

The Colonel's mind reeled under the news of his defeat. Then he disappeared, leaving no trace. Suicide was feared. Benjamin was summoned to Holland, and arrived in three days without stopping for either rest or food. After an interval of frenzied family consultation, the colonel was discovered to be lying dangerously ill at Bruges, though a letter from him, written to be delivered after his death, had already reached the Statholder. But the unhappy soldier rose from his death-bed with cries of vengeance, and decided to prolong his life, to obtain the revision of the verdict, the vindication of his honour, and the punishment of his enemies.

In this upheaval of his father's fortunes Benjamin displayed admirable devotion. He besought the Duke; he besought the Prince of Orange; he drew up portentous memorials for the Swiss authorities; he mastered the myriad technicalities of the thirteen lawsuits: he patiently sought to curb the excesses of violence whereby the injured colonel was ruining his chances of redress; he acted as peacemaker in the family broils which, as usual, followed close on family disaster. He understood Juste's helpless, solitary, and secretly tender nature; and he was consumed by a passion of loyalty for a father who, in twenty years, had seldom spoken to him without a sneer.

From the shores of Lake Neuchâtel Madame Charrière surveyed this drama with her customary detachment. Everyone was debating the pros and cons of the *procès Constant*. With her implacable addiction to truth, she sought to form a just view of the merits of the case. With her untimely sincerity she revealed her conclusions to Benjamin.

In her eyes Benjamin's sacred virtue was at stake—his integrity of thought. Had he said, "I am fighting for my father, right or wrong," she would have applauded his humanity. But he said, "my father is entirely in the right," when, in fact, Colonel Juste de Constant was demonstrably on certain points in the wrong. And this he must not say; at least not to her, his priestess of truth.

And so she allowed herself a laconic hint that the matter was not quite so simple; a tersely oracular hint.

The air between them had long been charged with storm. In Benjamin's nature the electricity was accumulated at a single point: loyalty to his grim father now meant more to him than any woman in

the world. The despotism of Colombier was insufferable.

He flashed out: "I am weary of your mysterious
ways of writing. I have no use for sibyls. . . . I retract
nothing; my father's conduct has been legal in every
case. . . . And with this I pray God keep you in His
holy care, and beg you urgently to burn all my letters.
Yours I burnt before I left Switzerland. I insist on
this as my right. It is for you to decide whether you
will release me from a source of anxiety, or punish
me for my past trust."

It was a lightning streak, suddenly illuminating,
and striking, the castle of friendship which she had
built and undermined.

Across the same sheet that Benjamin had used for
his ultimatum she wrote her haughty reply: "Write
to me—and sign it in full—that you have burnt *all*
my letters: I will then *immediately* burn yours. *I.A.E.
van Tuyll van Serooskerken de Charrière. Ce mercredi
23 septembre* 1789."

And then she reflected; and she added, "If you
have come to your senses before this reaches you, do
not worry about the effect of your rude and savage
outbreak: I shall have forgotten it sooner than you."

Then she took another sheet and wrote some more
in a kindly tone—small, disarming details of her
daily life, *comme si de rien n'était*. And then, with a
sting, she reminded him of sums of money which he
owed to Monsieur de Charrière—his failure to repay

them laid him open to ugly criticism: she "could judge of that by the effect it made upon herself."

And then she begged permission to keep a few of his letters and notes—"indifferent scraps of mere friendship, mere wit." And *one other* letter? . . .

And then she posted it all. And then she sent to the post office and got the letter back.

So it has remained, preserved among her own papers, a perfect record of femininity, a record of Madame de Charrière's pride, her gentleness, and her subjection.

She made peace. Benjamin's own words echoed in her mind: "One must love you, and submit."

XII

ZÉLIDE SAID OF HERSELF: "I AM LIKE A PORT,
or a market, for ideas. They come and they go.
I make them over, or I send them back; or I
lay them in store. All is in movement."

She must work and think, must analyse and demonstrate continually. She shut her love as far as possible out of sight. If it made havoc in the darkness she would not know it. Her energy and her will were busy loading and unloading the cargoes of her thought, packing and repacking and putting them to sea; little fleets; book, pamphlets, satires, and letters. Yet all she wrote was brief, impatient, disillusioned. She would invent no more romances. How, she asked, could anyone be expected to credit the characters of an ideal world, while the guillotine in France was at work dissecting the realities of human nature?

The Revolution was the one topic of those years. A stream of refugees sought safety at Neuchâtel, and often a crowd of them would be gathered in the garden at Colombier, lamenting their fallen fortunes, denouncing the Jacobins, or discussing the rise and fall of the exchange in francs. "They destroy the sentiment of pity," said Madame de Charrière, "or submerge it beneath their own folly. They show that the French nobility is nothing—a mere emptiness like the wind, a thing already over and past, and its oblivion already begun." To those that merited it her kindness was inexhaustible. But intellectually she found nothing to choose between the parties. "No one thinks of anything but politics," she wrote to a diplomat of her acquaintance. "I too sometimes think of them, but in a manner that satisfies no one. I cannot fully enough share the hopes of the convinced democrats, nor wring my hands like their adversaries. Neither my indignation, nor my applause, nor yet my advocacy, suffices for any one. And if I talk music instead of politics that, too, is unwelcome." In these circumstances she preferred to write rather than to talk. And while the groups of *émigrés* sauntered round the house, or called at her gate, Zélide sat apart in her room and composed "L'Aiglonette"—a fable on Marie Antoinette—and sent it through the post "to the Queen of the French." It was a sequel to her "Bien Né"—a fable on Louis XVI—which passed in Paris as the work of Mirabeau. She followed these by "Letters Found in the Snow" and "Letters from the Pocket Books of Exiles," and a comedy in three acts entitled "L'Emigré." If these terse writings lack inspiration or completeness they reveal an almost passionate commonsense and a kind of scornful moderation. The little party at Colombier, Mademoiselle L'Hardy, Mademoiselle Moula, Monsieur de Charrière himself, were kept busy transcribing the manuscripts, and sometimes one of the refugees would lend his hand. And, after that, good Herr Hüber would be called in to translate the work in German.

164

Louis Ferdinand Hüber was Madame de Charrière's latest acquisition. She liked queer, stray, human beings. Let ideas be sane, and human beings odd. "If I were a great lady, I would rather have a menagerie of odd people than one of peacocks, ducks, and monkeys with and without wigs." The waifs of the world—the eccentrics—were more to her taste than conventional men and women rubbed smooth by success. Waifs were more likely to have her "favourite virtues," sincerity and frankness. They were more teachable, too; they could be helped, looked after, and ruled. What was Benjamin, after all, but the queerest of her fishes?

Hüber was a worthy literary man who had been a friend of Schiller's. He had sunk through poetry to politics and now edited a newspaper entitled "Friedenspreliminarien." He had drifted to Neuchâtel with a very sentimental German lady, Thérèse Forster, whose husband had confided her to his earnest embraces. Forster was a traveller and a revolutionary; he had circumnavigated the globe with Captain Cook and was now occupied in putting it to rights. So engrossing was his political vocation that he was unable to cope with the demands of a wife whom he adored; he had lent her to Hüber, and the peculiarity of this union was disguised to the satisfaction of the parties concerned by a dense nebula of German sentiment. Madame Forster recalled "five marvellous, unforgettable days" passed with Hüber and Forster "in a wretched and rustic hut surrounded by snow-covered rocks" on the slopes of the Jura. But the society of Neuchâtel took a harsher view of the matter, and Madame de Charrière alone extended her protection to the struggling Hüber. She welcomed him to Colombier, recognized his conspicuous qualities of heart, encouraged his talent, endured for his sake the outpourings of Madame Forster, and set them both to work on the translation of her books.

Yet all this activity—this writing of books, this collecting of waifs—had no directing aim. It served to kill time; it helped her to forget the monotony of Colombier and the maddening passivity of Monsieur de Charrière to whose inert presence she was for ever chained; it blessedly shut out the carping tones of Mademoiselle Henriette and the cooing of Mademoiselle Louise; above all it prevented Benjamin from absorbing her thought and imagination. Her pride would not allow that a human centre was necessary to her happiness. She strove to hide from herself the truth that she was simply a childless, passionate, protective woman who had been frustrated in every instinct, and that the life of reason, which she had embraced so gallantly and defiantly at the start, was now no more than a makeshift and a screen. She wearied of Hüber; in her menagerie of odd people she had no intellectual equals; to think, in that prison of Colombier, was a constant and laborious miracle. She turned from topic to topic with flagging interest and a terribly unabated will. The wheels of her intellect revolved at random in a kind of busy void, and the conclusion was always the same: *à quoi bon?*

The Chevalier de Revel, envoy of Sardinia to the Hague, had a theory of the universe which fitted Madame de Charrière entirely. "God died," wrote Benjamin to Zélide, "before finishing His work. His plans were magnificent and vast; His means were immense. The scaffolding, so to say, of His resources and appliances was in some measure complete when He perished. Everything which now exists was created for an end which no longer has existence. Ourselves, in particular, are aware of a destiny we cannot define. We are like watches without a dial, and the wheels wear themselves out with turning. They are endowed with intelligence, and, as they turn, incessantly repeat: 'I turn, I turn: therefore I serve some end.' I far prefer," he adds, "this folly to those of the Christians, Moslems, and philosophers of the first, sixth, and seventeenth centuries. . . . Good-bye, most dear and intelligent Wheel, who have the misfortune to be so superior to the clock you are part of, the clock that you derange."

Benjamin, in fact, was beginning to discern that Zélide had "deranged the clock." He wanted her tenderness; she persisted in giving him her "understanding." He was weary of her philosophy: it was too like his own. His pessimism had ceased to be an intellectual toy; the reality of it had begun to frighten him. Benjamin was an hereditary pessimist—the Constants were born black. Nurtured in blackness by the colonel's sarcasm, he had been confirmed in it by the agitations of his boyhood, by his futile life at court, by the crash of his father's fortunes, and by the misery of his marriage with Wilhelmina. Who could live with Wilhelmina? She was plain, vulgar, and unfaithful; and she kept pets.[1] He was formally separated from her in March 1793; and Minna signed an acknowledgment that there were "grievous faults" on her side, and that "M. Constant had behaved laudably in every detail throughout the course of their differences, and that anything said to the contrary is false."

And, characteristically, five days after the deed of separation was signed, he wrote: "For more than a year I have waited for this moment, and longed after my freedom. It has come, and I shudder at it. I am aghast at the solitude that surrounds me; I am full of fear, with nothing to hold to—I, who have complained so long at being held."

He was nearing the crisis of his inner life. The philosophy of disillusion, that he had trifled with in his long intercourse with Madame de Charrière, descended now, a veritable darkness. Even his literary

[1] This propensity found free play after her divorce. In 1813 she had one hundred and twenty birds, two squirrels, six cats, eight dogs, and some other unassorted animals such as magpies, crows, fish, etc. All these lived together in a single but fortunately large room.

ambition failed him. Still, in his black fatalism, his
mind keeps analysing rightly: on the edge of complete despair a struggle begins in him against his own
aloofness, egoism, irony. Not long after this date he
writes to Madame de Nassau de Chaudieu: "Think
of my education, my wandering and shapeless life,
the endless appeals made in childhood to my vanity,
the tone of irony that is the style of my family, its pose
of flippancy where feeling is concerned, its refusal to
value anything but brilliancy and fame: can you wonder that I was shaped to this way of being? It has cost
me too much suffering not to renounce it. I have
learnt too clearly that in standing aside and seeing
nothing but the absurdity of things one touches no
depths. The pleasure of self-esteem is not worth a
moment of real feeling. I am tired of my own mockery, I am tired of surrounding my heart with a mist
of dismal indifference that shuts me out from every
experience of happiness. . . . Give me rather the
folly of enthusiasm."

The way is opening for Madame de Staël. The will
to act and to trust is awakening. But still he pleaded
with Madame de Charrière, his mistress in disillusion; still he looked to her for a few generous and
vital lies and for a less diffident affection. "Send me
nectar; I send you dust. I have nothing else to send.
I am entirely dust." But she sent him irony, she
teased him with advice, and reminded him of his
debts to Monsieur de Charrière: "I have been clumsy

indeed," she replied, "if I have merited your reproach of being hard when you are tender, and tender when you are hard. . . . Perhaps I have been more frank with you when I saw you return to your old self, more reserved and ceremonious when I thought I must go carefully or lose you altogether. I assure you that there has been no contrary movement of my heart, no single feeling of severity towards you since we parted. . . . Ah, Sire, how difficult it is to speak frankly to Your Majesty without offence. And yet, what Majesty in the world is better able to stand the searchings of the most rigorous frankness than a Majesty as witty, as wise, and as lovable as Yours? Why does that Majesty refuse my humble advice, which amounts to so little, and, coming from so far, strikes so feebly at its aim? Would you, Sire, be offended (for example) if I were to ask you again for the note that Monsieur de Charrière charged me months ago to obtain from you—a business note, in such few words? You cannot know how much it hurts me to see you placed in a false position among those with whom I live. They are tactful and say nothing; but I understand their meaning too well."

Nevertheless, when Benjamin came to pass the winter of 1793 at Colombier, the clouds between them vanished. The friction of correspondence ceased, the delight of intimacy was renewed. The reconciliation seemed complete.

Benjamin, unwilling to increase his obligations to Monsieur de Charrière, lodged himself and his library of 1500 books at the old feudal castle across the road, but his time was passed at the manor house. Here he formed a close friendship with Hüber, who—Forster having conveniently died—was now duly married to his lady.

Madame Hüber, recalling this winter, has left three clear pictures of Madame de Charrière, of Benjamin, and of herself. "Madame de Charrière," wrote this insufferable but observant woman, "was *so like myself* that the excessive similarity of our natures precluded a close sympathy. In 1793, and for long afterwards, she was my idol and the object of my passion. We did our best to be intimate, we admired and understood each other, but like certain electric currents we were mutually repelled." One can picture the process.

"This woman," the German lady continues, "was an enchantress when she pleased, or where her affections were concerned. Benjamin Constant was her last love. . . . When I knew her she was weary of society; the timid mediocrity of those around her, the resistance she everywhere encountered—even at home, her tastes, habits, opinions, and the repeated disillusionments of her heart—all this had made her difficult. Her judgments were entirely fearless, but she kept within certain strict limits imposed by French convention. Her spirit was vital, despotic, magnanimous, and always noble even when she was most unjust; I have never known an equal nobility. Her activity was ceaseless, her mind was trenchant, her way of expressing it was often cynical; but she was irresistible when she wished to charm."

And now Benjamin: "Constant," she writes, "was infinitely lovable, a libertine without corruption. He is not domestic, orderly, or active. He can most easily do without everything; he can sew the buttons on his own shoes like a little clerk and make his own soup. He is full of learning, and feels a ceaseless need of occupation. With all these contrasts he could yet recognize, not without sadness, the worth of our simple and pure domestic bliss. Like Abadonna at the gates of heaven he looked on with a silent grief at the happiness of Hüber and myself.

"He is tall, and there is a certain grace in his awkwardness, and something distinguished in his ugliness. With his mottled complexion and red hair—(I have always loved red hair since)—he has an air of youthful vitality. He is a failure, and broken by life, but so finely gifted that the divine seal has never been quite effaced. Madame de Charrière found him in Paris, ruined by his childish and ingenuous prodigality. . . . She saved his life by her devoted care."

And "My heart beat," Madame Hüber adds, with a Teutonic touch, to recognize the delicate love which subsisted between Benjamin and Madame de Charrière despite their difference of years, and "my eyes sought out in surprise the eyes of Hüber. It was a strange thing, contrary to my sentiment and my principles; and yet I felt it."

No records remain of Benjamin's visit until we come to his letters of farewell. They show him completely once more under the sway of Zélide. He began to dream of settling at Colombier. "It is only on to you that my mind can come to rest," is the refrain. "I love you: it is with you alone that I find happiness. . . . You alone in the world are utterly fitted to me." And Zélide had, for once, so clearly revealed the force of her own attachment, that Benjamin, who knew how much she hated to show an emotion, had slipped away at the end without good-byes, leaving a letter and his key to the house.

She wrote, "I was in no way angry; I divined your intention and was grateful for it; but I was struck rigid with surprise—all except my fingers, for Muson (Mademoiselle Moula) told me the same evening that I worked at my festoons like the wind. . . . I read your letter many times, and I noticed the very needless words 'please love me' with pleasure: I counted how often they were used, and all you wrote was read in the same spirit. Only on one point you were wrong. 'Last evening did you no good: to-night will be worse," you said. . . . On the contrary, I shall remember that evening for the rest of my life as a sequence of precious hours. You, idly seated; I, lying down with the moon striking on the end of my long *couchette*; our slow and gentle talk; I see and hear it all. These last days, and that evening, I have been struck by the truth, the sincerity, and fairness of your judgment which rejects no light that can be thrown on matters that you seem normally to approach with some passion of prejudice. I have sometimes accused you of refusing to revise your first impressions; and no, you show an amazing patience in your return to the appreciation of men and things. . . . You cannot live far from me, nor I without you. I know that in theory and the eyes of the world, things cannot be equal between us. And yet—what is to be gained by thinking of that? . . . Come back! No one loves or understands you as I; no one prizes you so deeply or truly; and if I die, as in nature I must, before you, then you can form other habits; there is no need to form them yet. . . . Good-bye, Constantinus."

How significant that in this moonlit parting, one thing should be chosen as for ever memorable— Benjamin's truth, his integrity of intellect.

So in April 1794 Benjamin left for Brunswick. And for some weeks they noticed that Zélide lay sunk in lethargy. Then she roused herself. The great avenues of elms in the village were in leaf; in the hollow, where the manor lay hidden, the scents of summer heavily drifted; the air was full of sound and secret movement. The sleep of Monsieur de Charrière was undisturbed in the old house, and about him his sisters moved in their death-in-life. But Zélide is alive, and never before had the future seemed so serene. Reason and emotion had made terms. At last she felt assured that Benjamin needed her; for eight years he had said it; now she would believe him. Had she dismissed her own story as an ill-written play, unfinished, without plot or plan? Now in middle life she saw the meaning and the motive. She felt towards Benjamin a quiet and immeasurable benevolence.

Zélide is right; the play is never finished. The lowered curtain will rise on another act. Another actor is waiting in the wings.

Enter Madame de Staël.

XIII

IT IS SUMMER, IN 1794. A HAZY LIGHT QUIVERS over the stretched lake of Geneva, and on and on, monotonously. A carriage has halted by the wayside near Nyon, in the dust of a September afternoon. Through the window a lady, dressed in black, has looked out: her black and burning gaze inspects the lanky figure of a young man striding on the Lausanne road. It is, beyond doubt, the figure—it has the stoop, the red hair—of Benjamin Constant; beyond doubt the eyes fixed upon him are the large and legendary ones of *Madame l'Ambassadrice*; the pair have recognized each other aright.

It is strange that they have not met before, for they have frequented the same world; and indeed, Benjamin explains, he is at this moment on his way back after paying a call of politeness at Coppet. Madame de Staël overflows, on that, with phrases so friendly and so compelling, that he forgets her formidable contours, her coarse face: she is a voice. And, forthwith, the voice of Madame de Staël invites him to mount and be seated beside her in the barouche. "She will carry him to Lausanne."

She will carry him to Lausanne; to Coppet, to Paris, to Weimar. She will carry him on the turbulent tide of all that speech out in the storms of her infinite ambition, launch him into the struggle with Napoleon, drive him over the adventurous chart of politics to fame and the Tribunat. She will carry him—by whatever necessary hurricanes of fury and downpour of tears—to her own region of wordy romance, away from scepticism and from diffidence and from the clear honesty of the mind, away from the eighteenth century and from Madame de Charrière.

And as he clambered into the coach, the spirits of irony watching over Benjamin reflected that Madame de Charrière herself had begged him in curiosity to meet Madame de Staël, had urged him on the road to Coppet. . . .

For what had Zélide to fear from the Ambassadress? Madame de Staël was the exact opposite of all that she prized in Benjamin, the opposite of all that Benjamin was accustomed to prize in others. He could be drawn by a mind dry and clear as his own—the magnet of Zélide; or, again, he could be decoyed by *une femme douce*, like Madame Johannot or Minna von Cramm. Madame de Staël filled neither of these roles: she was cloudy and overbearing, a blend of tyranny and gush. Benjamin had talked of her at Colombier. He had mocked, a score of times, at Madame de Staël's reputation, her pretensions, and her prose. In every legend of her triumphs he had laid his finger on the vulgar blemish; in everything she had written he had detected the false note. *"C'est à cracher dessus,"* he had said.

And then one day Madame de Staël had come to Colombier to see the author of "Caliste."

At this moment Madame de Staël was engaged in mourning her mother, Susanne Curchod. Or rather, she had settled in Switzerland to console Monsieur Necker, her father and "guiding star," in the loss of his wife. For Germaine de Staël had never hit it off with her pedantic mother, while she worshipped the great financier with a fervour which, she averred, was only equalled by her passion for ideal causes. "God, Liberty, and Monsieur Necker" came first, a shining trinity, in a supreme sphere of adoration; her lovers were placed in a second fiery region; and Susanne Curchod had to be content with the leavings of her daughter's sentimentality. And now Susanne—the ex-governess who had preached by the wayside from little arbours of trellised foliage, who had loved and been deserted by Gibbon, and had married the millionaire Necker and ruled over the most solemnly intellectual salon in Europe—Susanne was dead; her body was preserved in a chemical fluid; it lay in a coffin with a glass window, and Monsieur Necker was living with it at Coppet.

German pathos of this kind was odious to Madame de Charrière. She was profoundly simple in matters of emotion, invariably and quietly responsive to any other's grief, respectful of family affection. But this was too much. The whole Necker world was insufferable. Deep down Madame de Charrière was still a van Tuyll, very proud of her simplicity. The display of parvenu wealth excited her disdain. Instinctively she had surrounded herself with unassuming folk—a world of hidden country people, and then Benjamin. If dignity were needed, let it be the dignity of lonely Zuylen, where the long generations had passed, unwatched, like shadows on the dial. The progress of the Neckers had been public, breathless, and absurd. Their intellectual pomp jarred on her no less than their social pretension. If brilliance were needed, let it be a private indulgence, like her talks with Benjamin, a festivity of friends. Madame de Staël had been exhibited from her first childhood, the prodigy of the Necker salon; she was now what Madame de Charrière most detested, a confirmed exhibitionist, and must have all Europe for witness. So Madame de Charrière fidgeted with discomfort at the prospect of enduring Madame de Staël's examination. She sat very erect in the quiet vaulted room at Colombier, and with the severity of a van Tuyll she received the advances of the Ambassadress.

Madame de Staël had come reverently, ingratiatingly—almost timidly. "Our Lady of Colombier" was known to be excessively formidable, and one could not go too carefully. There had been compliments on the subject of "Caliste"; Madame de Staël had read "Caliste" ten times; this was true, as became evident when, later, she herself wrote "Corinne." But Madame de Charrière received the flattery with suspicion. Then had followed cajoleries about the mysterious authorship of "Mistress Henley"; "It is only in Holland, I think, that true French can be acquired," Madame de Staël had sonorously said; and Madame de Charrière had been stonily acquiescent.

For, however much Madame de Staël might cajole or Madame de Charrière be polite, the air of the little room was electric with antipathy. They knew each other, these two *femmes fortes*. There was in the air the contempt of the thinker for the rhetorician, the impatience of the classic for the romantic, the scorn of the aristocrat for the parvenue—of the great lady whose choice was to live obscurely among peasants for the Ambassadress who had never learnt manners. The deep pride of tradition confronted the arrogance of success; the assurance of youth challenged the assurance of age. And the older woman hated the younger.

Madame de Charrière eyed the Ambassadress narrowly, scanning the thick too powerful figure, and meeting the dark penetrating gaze that redeemed the coarse-bred features. And reluctantly she admitted—for she was always just—that the impression was one of beauty.

And "how well she talks," reflected Madame de Charrière. Yes, her talk was indisputably much better than her prose; such precision, such flow, such beauty of diction and of cadence, such quick initiative, such readiness and fitness in reply—when had

these been found together? Against her will Zélide
acknowledged an interest, a curiosity, in this new and
vital and shocking force. She reflected that Benjamin
had done Madame de Staël less than justice. . . .

"I am still of your opinion," she wrote to Benjamin, "Madame de Staël's brilliance is false, and all
her 'feelings' are mere brilliance. But you must hear
her talk."

Her speech was amazing, and that was all. So much
Madame de Charrière had been willing to concede,
but she had not unbent. Madame de Staël had continued to lay siege to Colombier. Her letters were
irritating. She spoke of settling at Neuchâtel. In a
world of despair, with Napoleon giving anxiety, with
Monsieur Necker widowed and in exile, what was
there to hold one to life, "what but the hope of
seeing Madame de Charrière?" she had fulsomely
written. But the more deferentially Madame de Staël
flattered, the more scrupulously Madame de Charrière withdrew. The Ambassadress was piqued, and
then her manners fell short of the punctilio a van
Tuyll required. "I have no further use for her,"
wrote Madame de Charrière, "if she thinks that fine
phrases will serve instead of correctness."

Zélide was in a hurry to share her impressions with
Benjamin. She was interested, in spite of her dislike.
"You must certainly see her," she urged him again

and again. "I am impatient for you to meet her. I long to hear what you will say." And so she sent him to Coppet.

And then came Benjamin's letter describing his encounter on the Lausanne Road. "I drove with her from Nyon. I supped, breakfasted, dined, supped, and breakfasted again with her." . . .

Did a faint, ominous rumble—the first premonition of disaster sound in Zélide's ear, in this list of shared repasts? I do not think so. She was too confident that this pretentious and unsubtle prodigy must offend Benjamin's fastidious mind. She did not guess that, released from Colombier, he was craving for vigour and action and hope.

Then, three weeks later, came the thunderclap. Benjamin wrote. "As for me, I have latterly had the happiness of turning away from sterile sensations, and I do not care to struggle with the past now that the future, as I believe, has still a hope for me. . . ."

What did this mean? What, or who, was the sterile "past"; what, or above all who, the "future"? The rest of the letter left no doubt. "Far from feeling it an effort to find 'praises to throw to Madame de Staël'" (this was rapped out in rebuke to a phrase of Zélide's) "it is with difficulty that I refrain from extolling her extravagantly to every one. . . . I have seldom seen such astonishing and attractive qualities in combination, such justice of mind united to brilliance, such an active flow of goodwill, such generosity, such gentle and unfailing politeness in society, so much charm, simplicity, and self-abandonment in intimacy. She is the second woman I have known who could have counted to me more than the whole world, who could have been a world to me in herself; you know who the first was. . . . In short, she is a being apart, a superior being, such as is found perhaps once in a century, and those who have access to her, who know her, and are her friends, must ask no other happiness."

Rapture: but perhaps there is as much cold deliberation as rapture in this letter. There is a hint of studied cruelty in its phrases of covert rebuke. There is a conscious crescendo, leading up to that deadly sentence: "she is the second woman I have known." It is an act of surgery, and a profession of faith.

"I am impatient for you to meet her: I long to know what you will say." Well, he had told her. This was much more than an amatory adventure; this was his judgment. Benjamin had reached, and knew that he had reached, the dividing of the ways. To confess allegiance to Madame de Staël was to disown his entire philosophy of life. It was to exchange his old aloofness and irony for her fervid convictions; to accept the adventure of living, and abandon its analysis. Madame de Charrière and Madame de Staël were the opposite poles of his universe. He was tired of playing Hamlet and would fain play Brutus.

His Hamlet-life had been shared and shaped by

Madame de Charrière. So completely had she owned
it that if he denied that life he must deny her too. She
was "the sterile past."

Yet the habit of intimacy was so strong that even
this renunciation was something which Zélide must
be made to understand and approve. His letter concluded: "I am impatient to see you."

Madame de Charrière measured the full magni-
tude of her defeat. "Stay where you are, dear Constantinus," she replied with characteristic simplicity
and control, "stay where you are. The weather is not
at all fine at Colombier, when it is fine at Mézery and
Lausanne. . . . I embrace you tenderly."

But those onlookers, Pastor Chaillet and Mademoiselle Henriette and the rest of her little world,
did not fail to perceive that the weather at Colombier
was disturbed. There was a sense of stifled thunder.
And to Mademoiselle L'Hardy, Zélide permitted
herself one solitary, terribly human outbreak of spite
and disdain. "Do you agree with the countess who
called Benjamin ugly? Red hair, little eyes like glass
and a discoloured face? Come now, agree, let us have
no prejudices. Were I madly in love with a man, still
I would wish to see him as he was." Then she pulled
herself up, and "*d'ailleurs*," she added, "*c'est plat
pour les hommes, d'être beaux.*"

The links which eight years had forged were slow
and painful in breaking. Benjamin, on his side,

hoped to keep her devotion. He asked only to be lib-
erated from her despotism; he refused to be her "sat-
ellite"; he must be free to think his own thoughts—
or the thoughts of Madame de Staël. But he would
neither renounce the affection of Zélide, nor withdraw his own.

She saw that he was asking the impossible. "To belong to Coppet and to Colombier and to Germany is
to belong nowhere," she insisted. She had never
admitted jealousy of Benjamin's loves; but, all the
more, she clung to her intellectual sway, and this
could not be divided. If he took the road to Coppet
she could not follow him with her thoughts: his fineness in her eyes would be gone; she saw clearly that
it was already gone. Then, very humanly, despite her
fixed purpose to withdraw from any semblance of
competition with Madame de Staël, Zélide, touched
by his insistence, wavered at the last. "You are no sat-
ellite," she wrote, "shine as much as you will with
your own light; but do not travel the heavens without me." She hoped they might still find some companionship, at least in their writings. "Write your
'Lettres Persanes' now," she said—comparing him
to Montesquieu—"you will have time for an 'Esprit
des Lois' when I am dead. I had looked forward to
seeing you finish something. Here I could understand you and follow you. If the task be not too great
I could help you, with criticism or in any way you

like. If you wish me to write something for your amusement, say so; I will do it so as to please you if I can."

He came to Colombier. But the topic of Madame de Staël, on which he cruelly insisted, provoked them to bitterness and reproach. The edifice they had built was visibly in ruin. And then, "Constantinus, let us make peace," she said, stretching out her hand.

He left her on that; but eight days passed without a letter from him, and she understood that he was at Coppet, too tactful to write to her *de chez Monsieur Necker*. She, who had possessed him fully, could not face a friendship of dissimulation.

For her part she would dissimulate nothing. She chose that her last letters should be simple and sincere. "I could not quickly forget," she wrote. "The experiment you practised upon me, above all in the famous eulogy of Madame de Staël; it made me jerk to think of it. . . . I did not accuse you of cruelty: a child will tear off the wings and legs of a fly without wishing to hurt. . . . I hoped I could submit; something, I hoped, might survive, however different to before. I worked myself up into thinking I would write new 'Calistes,' or what not, simply for your entertainment. In writing to you I did my best to add softness and modest ornament to that bare style of mine which you have blamed." (An infinitely pathetic attempt to conciliate him by imitating Madame de Staël.) "Had our views been alike my letter would have displeased you; you found it charming; and I, who had written it with that sole object, was angry with my success and with your praise. . . . I concluded that our intimacy is a finished thing, and that its death, with all that may come after, must be taken lightly and in good part. I had suffered too much, and must protect myself from the sleeplessness, the palpitation, and the despair which every line of yours has for some time caused me. . . .

"You will say that to keep you at such a distance is to lose you altogether; for me, above all, for whom what is not everything is nothing. Perhaps: but the thing is done and it is not of my doing. . . . To my unhappiness I find you changed. Your smoothed hair, your yellow trousers, your perfume, yesterday's letter with its amber scent, each dealt a stab. You may for all I know be more likeable, but you are no longer what you were. Even the change in your politics hurts me . . . you are all of a sudden a Tallieniste, a Talleyrandist, and who knows what else. . . . So much the better."

She would indulge in no quarrel, no dramatic rupture, no scenes in the manner of Madame de Staël. Out of piety for the past she kept the last threads unsevered, and to the end she wrote him, at rare intervals, letters that were most often brief statements of fact. (The last letter she dictated before death was to Benjamin, telling him of her grave illness—a fact, like another.) But she refused Benjamin's plea for the renewal of their intimacy. He could not serve two goddesses; he had chosen the false mysticism of Germany: the doors of the temple of reason were shut and the altar of Colombier would never be rekindled.

When she had most prized his devotion she had wounded it by her hardness, induced by a stoical recognition of that barrier of age between them, of which Benjamin thought so little and she, perhaps, so much. Now that she closed her heart finally against him, her tone was gentler than ever before. "I have no resentment, Constantinus," she wrote. "I am neither difficult nor easy by halves." Yet the words seemed to him to come from behind an impenetrable barrier across unmeasured deserts.

And suddenly in one of these external letters—in the midst of a request on behalf of Monsieur de Charrière for the services of Benjamin's valet, Christian—a phrase revealed the thought that lay beneath: "*There is in my detachment from you enough to make one of the finest attachments in the world.*"

"I am grateful to Christian," replied Benjamin, "for having caused us to interchange letters. . . . Your handwriting, and the few words you let slip, are a joy for me. I would have asked you to keep Christian, hoping by this small sacrifice to convince you of what you refuse to believe:—that I shall never cease to love you, that, though I may have been deeply wrong in my manner of acting—for my character is both harsh and inconsequent, my heart has never varied, and that I am held to you by every memory, by every regret, and I would like to add—in spite of you—by many a hope.

"Good-bye, you who enriched eight years of my life, who in spite of bitter experience I can never picture as formal or estranged, you whom I know how to value better than anyone will value you ever. Good-bye; good-bye."

XIV

THE CIRCUMSTANCES OF LIFE AT COLOMBIER were always hateful to me; *I never came back to the place without a sense of despair. I determined then never to leave it.* And I have rendered it endurable."

So Madame de Charrière once wrote to Benjamin, and the sentence gives the key of her character. At every critical turn of her life instinctively she chose the more stubborn alternative and rendered it endurable by a grim completeness of acceptance. She was intolerant of suspense, of half-measures, of losing battles; almost she was intolerant of hope. Hope, the soft encouragement of a faith which the facts do not warrant, offended the clear logic which was the only faith she knew.

Her decisions were quiet and stoical, but extreme. At the close of her agitated youth in Holland, after its wild rebellion against the narrow decorum of the van Tuylls, had she not coldly envisaged marriage with the ferocious Lord Wemyss as an alternative to taking vows as a Carmelite nun? "*I determined then never to leave it,*" she would have said; and made reasonable terms, we may be sure, with the Earl or the Abbess. To have joined her life with her brother's mathematical Swiss tutor may have seemed to her, looking back over the years, a no less extreme step; but she accepted Monsieur de Charrière at her side as she accepted the Alps. It is recorded that for fif-

teen years she never took a walk outside the walls
of his garden. "By nature I am as variable as you,"
she added in the same letter to Benjamin, "and I am
capable of being affected far more deeply; by force
of will and endurance I have found cure and steadiness."

From under the tiles of the sleepy manor house
Zélide looked across the hills that shut the road to
Coppet. A few miles away, irreparably far, was Benjamin with his scented hair, his new mannerisms
—the fastidious Benjamin, ridiculously revolving
round Madame de Staël, competing with her court
of lovers, capping her epigrams, or gauchely taking
part, dressed in wreath and toga, in those ceaseless
theatricals. For the Ambassadress must have her
stage in emulation of Voltaire, and Benjamin must
strut to her bidding. The image was too distinct; like
that other image of Madame de Staël herself with her
perpetual turban, her negroid beauty, her masculine
strength, her hysterical quarrels and all too vividly
passionate reconciliations. . . . And Zélide would
take from her table the latest book of *la trop célèbre*,
and turn its pages and read a few sentences until she
met the fatal patch of insincere rhetoric, the inevitable twist of affectation, the rant, the strained an-
tithesis. Had Benjamin passed this, or praised that?
If so he must indeed be blinded, or else miserable.
Surely miserable. And what was this? Madame de
Staël speaking of "*la posterité contemporaine.*" What

could anyone be expected to make of such a phrase? Contemporary posterity—*quel amphigouri! quel galimatia!* And Zélide closed the book with classic disdain.

But the phrase was true. Madame de Staël was indeed "posterity"—she spoke with the new tongue of Romanticism, of enthusiasm, of confidence and belief. She was opening for Benjamin the avenues of the future, when he was weary of scepticism. She spoke the tongue of the nineteenth century, the tongue that Zélide was too proud to understand. And Madame de Staël was "contemporary"; she was alive; she had confronted the eighteenth century; she had crossed the path of Zélide; she had taken away her man.

It was better to think of other things. Surely "by force of will and endurance" one could think of other things. Of the querulous ejaculations of Monsieur de Charrière, of the sour looks of Mademoiselle Henriette, of the platitudes of Mademoiselle Louise? For thirty years she had lived with these, and of these how long ago she had ceased successfully to think! Should one think of politics—of the events in France? Madame de Charrière detested the strife of parties; her moderation and shrewdness were offended by the clap-trap of liberty no less than by self-praises of the *ancien régime*. Liberty—the eighteenth Fructidor! That was the work of Madame de Staël, the new work of Benjamin. Madame de Charrière stood gallantly for reason, and resolutely she wrote her sensible books. "Trois Femmes," a novel on the idea of duty, was published in a mutilated form in England because its morality scandalized the Duchess of Devonshire; at Vienna it was placed upon the Index. She wrote on and on. She composed "Asychis, or the Prince of Egypt," a novel on the education of rulers, and "Sir Walter Finch and his son William," a novel on the education of plain men. They are difficult to read, these later reasonable books, plans for the bettering of this or that, cold pleas for good sense delivered drily and without hope, the bric-a-brac of her disenchanted mind.

She wrote now swiftly, constantly, carelessly, without regard for literary fame. She devised her books simply in order that Hüber might translate them into German, to help poor Hüber to make money. In the last resort, here, she considered, was a reasonable occupation—to help Hüber. Her mind, which destroyed everything, could find no fault with that. By philanthropy, "with endurance," one could find "cure and steadiness."

This it was that gave Madame de Charrière the aloof, alarming quality that even her deep benevolence came to possess. Zélide had questioned happiness from the first, seeking only for life; and life had escaped her and dwindled to nothing beneath the search of her mind; she no longer sought life: she sought only to create routine, and to endure it. Even her infinite acts of kindness had something frightening about them, in the chill of her self-control.

Closing the door against Benjamin, she who had always been lonely saw herself, at last, alone. She seemed to those around her like one moving in an empty room.

They compared her to Madame du Deffand. Like Madame du Deffand she would sit and talk with a clear swiftness, and there was a screen between her and those that listened, like that screen of blindness.

But, in these last years, it was to very different listeners than the brilliant world of Madame du Deffand that she spoke. Incapable herself of self-deceit, she would not allow others to flatter themselves with any illusions born of vanity or pretence. She nipped every catchword and every artifice. Pomp, prudery, and paradox shrivelled in that clear sharp air. All who dealt in these avoided her. This was as she wished.

She preferred to play Providence to the obscure folk who had drifted to Colombier as the stray leaves drifted in from the courtyard. For the most part they were women. There was Henriette L'Hardy, handsome as a Van Dyke, on whom Monsieur de Charrière from behind his folio of mathematics would sometimes covetously peer. There was Isabella de Gélieu, a romantic dark-eyed beauty of peasant stock with a gift for poetry. There was Marianne Ustrich, an Austrian girl abandoned by her parents, who was discovered keeping a herd of goats in a forest and reading the "Télémaque" of Fénelon. And there was always modest Mademoiselle Moula who, year after year, cut out her black paper silhouettes. These Madame de Charrière untiringly taught, counselled, and protected. She advised them in their love affairs, and guided them in their fortunes. But the conversation of such ladies was subjected to a despotic discipline. "For some time past," wrote Zélide, "I have advised every woman to study logic. I have learnt from the *émigrés* how necessary it is to have the habit of strict reasoning in order not to fall into vulgar fallacies the moment we are tempted to do so by any motive of pain or resentment, or when new circumstances contradict old habits. Mademoiselle Moula has been docile to my preaching, and I find her marvellously improved. For the last six weeks I have hardly heard a single unreasonable expression of surprise or of unwarranted credulity. She no longer affects to understand what is obscure; she begins to understand what is clear. She is now reading Locke. If good sense could become fashionable, it would be the happiest of modes."

And, indeed, the little group of dependents at Colombier flourished happily enough on this austere treatment. Madame de Charrière tempered her logical doctrine with humour and practical generosity.

"If she had her way," wrote one of her protégées, "she would strip herself of her last possession." "I love you with all my heart and soul," wrote Madame de Madeweiss, "in fact with such love as—if one did one's duty—one ought only to give to God." All sought her advice; her assistance came unobtrusively, unsought. In their midst, Madame de Charrière, with her own thoughts veiled in silence, reigned aloof, a feared, benignant idol.

Proudly she narrowed her life, training her energy to the smallest task and her sympathy to the homeliest peasant. She liked to stress the contrast between Colombier and Coppet—Coppet where so many luminaries shone in planetary splendour, Coppet "the magic lantern of the universe." Away in France, scene after scene, the drama of the Revolution was enacted with the passionate participation of Madame de Staël. And sometimes Monsieur de Charrière would saddle his horse and ride in Neuchâtel for the latest news, and perhaps bring back a copy of the "Moniteur" with an article by Benjamin, and with reluctant justice she would read it and admit that it was good. But she deeply distrusted the generalizations of politics, and the only dramas that convinced her of sincerity were the unwordy tragedies of the mute individual mind. Some of the outlaws who had fled from the Terror found her a tower of defence. On Camille de Rousillon, a young noble of boyishly romantic charm, she sought for a while to expend the despotic impulses of protection that could no longer find their outlet in Benjamin. The chivalrous Camille, she wrote, "is everything which we are asked to believe that every Frenchman is; but he is French, which for me is something of a fault"; and then, wistfully, she added to Benjamin: "You and I, in the days of our friendship were of no country."

Camille submitted with devotion to Madame de Charrière's authority. She laboured to teach him languages. "One must not," she said, be "too much of one's own land";—and "the French are accustomed to think that to call bread and wine anything but *pain et eau* is to distort the Nature of Things." But Camille de Rousillon, for all his grace, could not fill the role of Benjamin. And when he wrote innocently from Paris that he had found Constant "poor, poor young man, more in love than a boy of eighteen, and jealous as a tiger," when he added that the salon of the Embassy "where Constant spends eighteen hours a day" brought out his talents more brilliantly than Colombier, then Madame de Charrière crushed him as only she could crush. "I beg your pardon," protested Camille; but Madame de Charrière's view of French tact was fatally confirmed.

Monsieur de Salgas, too, made the mistake of mentioning that he had seen Benjamin at Rolle "on his way to Coppet." "I am not interested," returned Madame de Charrière, "in small news. Do I wear you with an account of all who pass through Colombier?" "It is the first time, I believe," murmured poor Monsieur de Salgas, "that I have so much as mentioned a passer-by." It was probably the last; and Monsieur de Salgas reflected again that his lifelong friend was "a very terrible lady."

Feared she had always been; deliberately she had kept the great world at bay. But even the simple, inarticulate folk whose love she desired feared her more than she suspected. Her servant girl confessed that when Madame de Charrière spoke she was "so confounded that sometimes she seemed to hear every word twice over, sometimes to hear several voices at once. All her senses were totally perturbed." Madame de Charrière was shocked at this discovery. "There is something in your voice," Mademoiselle Moula explained, "something indefinable in your look . . ." and added that she herself, after years of intimacy with Madame de Charrière, found herself frequently in the same predicament as Rosette.

The terror which Zélide unwillingly inspired became legendary. Her nephew, Guillaume de Tuyll, a boy of eighteen, visiting Colombier in 1799, wrote, "As I approached the sanctuary, I confess my heart was in my boots. I stopped in a forest of firs through which I had to pass, and said to myself 'What induces you to go on?' At last I summoned up enough courage to go to an inn from which I sent a note announcing my arrival. Madame de Charrière despatched a servant with so civil a reply that I had no choice but to proceed." But reality belied the legend. "I found her on the high road, coming to meet me. Nothing could have been kindlier than her welcome; she put me so much at my ease that I could not believe I was meeting her for the first time. We took supper out of doors. No words can tell the relief with which I said to myself: 'That meeting is over' . . ." Next morning "she was gay and made me laugh till I cried. I know no one who talks so well or so easily—without shade of pedantry or severeness."

Monsieur de Charrière sunned himself in brief propitious intervals like these. For Guillaume resembled Zélide's favourite brother, the dead sailor Ditie, and unlocked far memories of Zuylen. And before long Madame de Charrière is reading the Aeneid with Guillaume, one on either side of the fire with a duodecimo edition of the poet, and Monsieur de Charrière is enthroned between them with a folio Virgil and a dog upon his knees.

But it was seldom that her remote Dutch memories were kindled, and the years passed aridly. Ageing side by side lived Monsieur and Madame de Charrière, a whole universe apart; and often a visitor would turn from the house with relief, and, hearing the gate clang behind him, would feel that he was leaving a shut tomb.

And on Madame de Charrière's features, every year, the look of her race became more visible, the pride of those mute van Tuyll ancestors was drawn about her lips. No one dared to show a sign of sympathy. One evening her friend César d'Ivernois, the poet-mayor of Neuchâtel, found her suffering more visibly than usual from the strain of her solitude. "Shall I stay?" he asked, as the night closed in. "Let me send a line back to my house, and stay. Can I be of any help?" "Of no help whatever," replied Madame de Charrière icily, and was conscious in the shadows of her own scornful smile as she spoke. But César, unbidden, sent the message and remained; and Madame de Charrière, unanswering, was grateful. The nights were lonely at Colombier with the wind rattling in the gables, and Monsieur de Charrière muttering by the hearth.

"I have many private grounds of sadness," the old man wrote. "The world is crumbling around me. I cannot say *Impavidum ferient ruinae*."

XV

A DUTCH PICTURE, MADAME DE CHARRIÈRE IS seated in her upper room working with her maid in the stillness. A broad band of sunlight slants from the half-shuttered window in the corner and falls upon Henriette Monachan pondering, pen in hand, at the table; her mistress looks up, watching her from the shadow. Madame de Charrière has narrowed her life until the company of Henriette is all she asks.

Everything had seemed open to Zélide, with her courtly suitors, her ardour, and her fame. She had chosen the obscurity of an intimate ideal, and it had failed her. The clock ticked; Monsieur de Charrière sat below, alone, poring over his mathematics. Rhythmically, from the barn outside, came the sound of the threshers. It throbbed, and it ceased. Life went on, though it was threshed out. Madame de Charrière sat revising "Trois Femmes." "The first words of a complaint are checked on my lips and my soul takes strength in the silence which I impose on it." Henriette, with whom she spent her days, took down the words to her dictation.

Mistress and maid; here was a relation that suited Madame de Charrière's despotic benevolence. She taught Monachan the elements of Latin; she made her read Locke on the Human Understanding. She enjoyed, perversely and patiently, to pour out on Monachan the benignant rain of her own stored wisdom, which sometimes fell in hailstones on more brilliant company. The passion for teaching, which mars most of Madame de Charrière's dogmatic little novels, had shown itself early at Zuylen, and had grown stronger with years. She who had refused to know Voltaire and had been as ice to Madame de Staël, thought nothing too good for Henriette Monachan who applied her unwarped and trusting mind patiently to the study of Locke. These were Madame de Charrière's serenest intervals.

At night she was sleepless; she dreaded the hours when her mind could no longer be bridled and driven down safe paths but would roam free in a dark waste. She sat late into the night and, for companionship, wrote long letters to Chambrier d'Oleyres, the tight-lipped Prussian diplomat, or Prévost, the academician at Berlin. With scholars at a distance she liked to exchange small services and discuss small points. I possess a letter in which Prévost communicates to her his latest musical discovery—the words and air of a negro song from the plantations, taken down, with learned annotations, from the lips of a little girl in the Dijon mail. A life of small things, desperately compelled to fill every crevice of the day: to this Zélide, who hated littleness, had come. "I am like a rough child who has been set to play with a set of quills, a carved ivory ball, or a chariot drawn by fleas: the child plays for a moment, becomes weary, and smashes all his toys."

Most of the creeping hours were spent composing her books for Hüber to translate. Carelessly she spoke them, and, pale in the mixed light of the candle and the dawn, sat pretty Henriette Monachan taking down the chapters—Henriette with whom Benjamin on his visits used to be so gallant. And Henriette recognized the voice of her mistress speaking through the dialogue of the tale: "I thank my destiny that I have only had a small boat to steer, and that in steering it ill I drown no one but myself." . . .

But the fancies of Henriette, while her brows were knit over "The Human Understanding," strayed elsewhere; they were in the stables with Racine, Monsieur de Charrière's handsome coachman. For Racine had seduced her, and Henriette for the second time was about to scandalize the Canton of Vaud with an illegitimate baby.

In this domestic crisis Madame de Charrière displayed a zeal equal to that with which Madame de Staël saved her friends from the guillotine and braved the wrath of Buonaparte. A harsh and sanctimonious tyranny brooded in Switzerland over the victims of such tender lapses, and an edict of expulsion was in process against Henriette for her offence against public morals. For two years Madame de Charrière assaulted the civil and ecclesiastical authorities of the Canton to avert this puritanical decree. These were the issues which roused her to action; the destinies of Europe she ironically abandoned to Benjamin and Madame de Staël. In the small world over which she presided hypocrisy should find no mercy. And suddenly the long latent antagonism between her and Pastor Chaillet flamed out before the delighted eyes of the citizens of Neuchâtel. The Pastor thundered, smiting his pulpit. The laxity of local morals was a point on which he had shown himself peculiarly sensitive since his own relations with one of his flock had been made a subject of veiled reproach by the Synod of his Church. For years he had chafed at the freedom of speech to which he listened in the drawing-room of Colombier, and in the avenues of the orchard he had muttered with Mademoiselle Henriette dark censures and prognostics of eternal punishment. Indeed, he would long ago have shaken the dust of Colombier from his feet, for he piqued himself on his intolerance, were it not for his easy winnings at Monsieur de Charrière's card-table and the solid worth of Madame de Charrière's gifts. He had his vanity, too, as a man of letters, and liked to read her his compositions. But things had gone too far. Once already, four years ago, she had protected the tender Monachan and stood sponsor to the fruit of her sin. Now he delivered his ultimatum: the limb of Satan must be cast out. Madame de Charrière could chose: she must abandon Henriette Monachan, or lose his friendship for ever: Pastor Chaillet would forego his income from piquet and cross the threshold of Colombier no more.

She chose Henriette, and received the signed indignant farewell of "Chaillet, Servant of Jesus Christ." And Madame de Charrière, reading that dwarfish handwriting for the last time, remarked: "One cannot say like Master, like man."

Pastor Chaillet withdrew. In his copy of her play, "L'Emigré," "A gift from the author. One could do without it," he microscopically wrote. "*On s'en passerait*," reflected Madame de Charrière also, as this last figure vanished. True, the pastor's had been, for a quarter of a century, the acutest intelligence in her shut provincial life. *On s'en passerait*, nevertheless. And of that life itself what better motto could be found? Indifference and scorn had settled so deep within its silences.

The misadventure of the amorous Monachan displayed in a crude and sorrowful light the solitude of Zélide. What had she in common with the world of her choice? In her view the persecution of the Swiss authorities was an act of bigotry, the attempt to separate her from a devoted companion was a personal affront, the eager interest in the petty episode was a prurient chatter of old maids. Mademoiselle Henriette, of course, had played Grand Inquisitor, and Monsieur de Charrière's fatal likeness to Mademoiselle Henriette had been sadly evident: timidly, with stammering conventional phrases, he had sided with his two sisters. For even Mademoiselle Louise, usually so charitable, had gloated. "The secret investigations of Mademoiselle Louise have filled me with disgust, with unspeakable disgust. I have seen too much propriety in this house, and seen it filtering everywhere and destroying the very faculty of straight thinking." All the repressed scorn of a lifetime of isolation became visible in Zélide's gesture. She took her meals apart in her room, and left Monsieur de Charrière and his sisters to eat in righteousness. "Why should I be forced to eat with him? These are fractions of sentiment which I leave out, as merchants leave out the pence in a large bill."

And Zélide sat very upright in her small chamber with her head held high, like one of the portraits of her van Tuyll ancestors framed upon the walls at Zuylen.

"It is quite simple," she wrote to Madame de Sandoz-Rollin; "I feel no bitterness . . . but I expect nothing from others and shut myself in my own mind. And often I sit for an hour or two on end beside Henriette Monachan without either of us opening our lips."

Madame de Charrière's efforts to avert the sentence were unavailing. Henriette was expelled by order of the Supreme Consistory. Later she was permitted to return, married, and sank into destitution.

And when all the actors of the story are vanished, when Monsieur de Charrière and his prim sisters are utterly forgotten, when Zélide is but a legend, and the body of Benjamin Constant has passed through the streets of Paris in public funeral with ninety processions clamouring to bear his coffin to the Panthéon, Henriette Monachan will live on, carrying into a later world her memories and her poverty. Monsieur Godet recounts that old men he had spoken with could recall a shabby figure at Yverdon, with a reticule and an air of faint gentility: Henriette, with her dim lights of Latin and recollection of Locke, who had been familiar with the gay Benjamin and shared the loneliness of Zélide; painfully supporting old age on a dole accorded to her by the guardians of Yverdon in consideration of certain ailments, and in particular of a soreness in the eyes, contracted—she explained—long ago, when her mistress was accustomed to dictate her thoughts to her in the night.

XVI

ONE DAY IS LIKE ANOTHER AT COLOMBIER.
Older grows Mademoiselle Louise in the
vegetable garden, older Mademoiselle Henriette at the card-table, older Monsieur de Charrière
by the fire. They are drifting like dreams, so many
baskets have been filled, so many parties of piquet
have been marked, so many, so very many nods have
fallen from the *bergère* by the hearth. If Zélide's
mind could drift too, how well that would be, like a
dream, from a dream into a sleep. But the mind is
awake; thoughts grind upon thoughts; she is always
thinking, thinking of something else, never of herself
if she can help it, something practical is wiser. She is
so good, they all say; so kind, say Mademoiselle Louise and even Mademoiselle Henriette, out of their
dream.

As Monsieur de Charrière grew infirm, his wife allowed him to share her room, and to sleep there. But
his dream turned rather to Henriette L'Hardy, for
she was kind to him, too, and young and healthy and
handsome, and smooth to think about. The old
scholar had grown querulous and tottering and ag-
grieved. A short journey, his: life had taken no interest in him. What had he been but an accurate, punc-
tilious man? Reason had come too easily to him; he
had worn it not gallantly like a badge of allegiance,
but tamely as a suit of clothes; now reason had taken
its revenge and his mind groped confusedly in a mist

of self-pity. But the brain of Zélide, beside him in the upper room, is turning, turning, like a purposeless engine without pause. "If I did not believe in the immortality of the soul," Madame Hüber commented, "Madame de Charrière would prove it to me: the body is destroyed, but age has no power over her mind." They watched her, thinking, working: she appeared like a being of more heroic race, driven by some relentless, inexplicable energy.

She never willingly spoke of herself; but to Benjamin she wrote: "It seems to me that our house is wearing out, and that we ourselves are wearing out. It is a double cause of distress in a time of extreme cold or of excessive winds. I spent last night listening to the wind."

She lay, with Monsieur de Charrière stirring uneasily beside her, and planned small benefits for Hüber, for Madame de Sandoz or Madame Chaillet, new lessons for Thérèse Forster or Marianne Ustrich, new arguments or incisive dialogue for a pamphlet or a play; her mind, intent on these occupations dimly registered the body's pain. Afterwards, after death, they will cut the body and discover a long-seated malady; now she lies unplanned and listening to the wind.

The fame of Constant's oratory in the Tribunat reached the Lake of Neuchâtel. She read his speeches, and made her recantation. She wrote to him: "I find here force, courage, and capacity: I find everything I admire. So it is possible, after all, to shake off rhetoric *after forming the habit of it.* I did not believe this; but I do now."

She admitted that he had touched reality in spite of Madame de Staël: she could not allow that Madame de Staël had led him to it. Madame de Staël was still the unpardonable crime. She did not know how desperately Benjamin was struggling in that bondage, nor that he had written in his "Journal Intime": "It is ten years since my breach with Madame de Charrière. How easily in those days I broke any tie that was irksome to me. How sure I was that I could form new ones to my own liking. How fully I seemed to possess life: how different it now seems."

Dust. "I will show you fear in a handful of dust." Benjamin was obsessed by the fear of death: he had turned from his solitary thinking, and chosen the anodyne of action, ambition, and belief. His very features had changed, they told her; and indeed they will be cast soon in the mould of the nineteenth-century reformer, noble unreasonable, arrogant, inspired. Zélide's reason had registered life's fulness and its emptiness. Of itself it had furnished no motive and no delight. But, even now, she would not repudiate her pride of logic: she feared no conclusion; she only observed, and waited. She lay at night planning now no longer for herself but for that "menagerie of odd people," who looked up to her, and seemed so small beside her stature. Dwarfs.

There had been nothing dwarfish about Benjamin, even in his follies.

Again she wrote to him: "It is true that I am no longer gay. But my fate as it nears its end has ceased completely to interest me. I have never had a fixed plan, never an ambition. I wished first for one thing, then another. . . . I have never believed that destiny could be shaped. I have not expected too much of myself. My life and my memories have no unity: my plan of life had none. *With you it should and could be otherwise.*"

XVII

INCREDULOUS OF FELICITY, ZÉLIDE HAD HUN-
gered for life rather than happiness. What part
had happiness in the pattern of the mind? But
the ironic powers had called her too, like Benjamin,
to sit beside them and look down on a ghostly feast.
Patterns in the mind: all her life she had been drawing them.

There had been a radiance—that flame in her
which Hermenches said must warm the heart of a
Laplander—and in the chill of her mind it had vanished. At last nothing was left but lines, masses: an
intelligence and a character as impersonal as the Alps
of her exile. They are too big for their landscape,
they close in the little valleys in vast shadow, and a
harmless people find quiet profit on their slopes,
while the light fades quickly from their summits clear
and frozen in the slow hours before the dark.

The winter of 1805 had set in. A ruffled bird or
two, half numbed, came for food to the plank she
had placed outside her window. The marks of its iron
supports are there to this day. It amused her to feed
and study them, as long ago at her first coming she
had leaned over the insects busy in the lime. Insects
going to and fro, quarrels of birds, motes of life, hungry self-absorbed existences that have no pause or
doubt, remote things; like men, to watch, to wonder
at, and to feed.

It is Christmas; the window is shut. Fog from the

lake fills the courtyard where a few soaked and amber faded leaves of the vine still cling under the wall. The door beneath the tiled porch opens and shuts quietly, quickly; women pass in from the mist, Mademoiselle L'Hardy, Madame Chaillet-de-Mézerac, Madame Sandoz. They gather in the hall, whispering; to-morrow, they say, will be the end; and on their way to the upper room cast looks of grave conventional concern towards the old man who talks to himself in the corner of the hearth.

Before him the flames of the fire sink or shoot forth their unpredictable shapes. His eyes have grown vacant; but perhaps, as he watched those lawless changes, brief brightness, smouldering crack, utter extinction, there moved across his face a shadow of grieved surprise, and again the serenity of a mute patience. With this look he had lived; thus, in his own manner, surprisedly, patiently, he had sought to love. Dimly he knew that the woman he had failed to make happy lay dying in the room above. But the picture flickered in his mind; and now its features were those of a girl at Zuylen, and now those of Henriette L'Hardy. "*Afterwards*," he thought—in who knows what blurred and senile search for comfort—"Henriette may marry me." Again the picture is of a woman dying. But the careful mechanism, which the gods loved not, no longer yields its flawless beat: all is faltering in Monsieur de Charrière's mind, like the shadows on the hearth.

But she, in the upper room, is lucid, and the shape of the darkness steady. Even at Zuylen, when men had wondered at the glow of her spirit, Zélide had watched herself from an icy cage. The cage is opening: there is nothing beyond. For others she had been kindly; for herself, lying there, she had no lenience at all, but only a chill, clear memory to the last. Whatever phantoms passed before her she looked on with no self-pity, without luxury of regret. Facts: fate: mere images, cold as the ripple on the moat at Zuylen, brief as the wind there; images—Zélide with Hermenches in her thoughts, her brother home from the sea, Benjamin, and again Benjamin and a blankness—the dark before her no emptier than that void. The friends, who had not filled it, stole from her, unnoticed, in awe.

Living there, in her benevolence, she had towered over them. Now, more than before, they moved around her in fear. The solitude of her dying filled the house like a presence, more lonely than the dead.

The mind has drawn its pattern. The Portrait of Zélide: a frond of flame; a frond of frost.

BENJAMIN CONSTANT
Silhouette by Mlle. Moula, in the
possession of Mme. P. Godet

M. DE CHARRIÈRE
Silhouette by Mlle. Moula, in the
possession of Mme. P. Godet.

NOTE

The obscurity Mme. de Charrière chose in her life-time soon began to darken into "the iniquity of oblivion."

Few remembered that Zélide had lived, when in 1844 Gaullieur published in the "Revue Suisse" some fragmentary letters to her, written by Constant. These attracted the notice of Sainte-Beuve who devoted several of his *Lundis* to the subject of their friendship. But Gaullieur had not accurately classified the letters in his possession, and in later publications took many liberties with the text. Sainte-Beuve never had sufficient evidence to study, and made no very penetrating study of the evidence he had. His judgment, moreover, was warped by political prejudice against Constant.

Then, in 1906, M. Philippe Godet published at Geneva his massive work, "Mme. de Charrière et ses Amis," and gave her, for the first time, substantial reincarnation. He had many advantages for his task. A distinguished professor at Neuchâtel, where Mme. de Charrière had passed her exile, he was familiar with local traditions and had access to private archives. He spent twenty years in collecting the records; nor is it the least likely that further sources of information will be added to those he methodically explored. The figure in my book is built from his materials.

I ventured, with the late M. Godet's most generous encouragement, on my own reconstruction for three reasons. First, his volumes have long been out of print; they are very difficult to obtain, and are not, it appears, to be republished. Secondly, M. Godet approached the subject avowedly from the angle of Neuchâtel; his work is much more than a biography of Mme. de Charrière: it is an erudite study of the lives of many individuals of primarily local interest, and likely to that extent to deter an English reader. Lastly, my reading of the character is not quite his.

All I have done here is to catch an image of her in a single light, and to make from a single angle the best drawing I can of Zélide, as I believe her to have been. I have sought to give her the reality of a fiction; but my material is fact.

To draw the portrait of Mme. de Charrière involves drawing the portrait of Benjamin Constant as she knew him: a picture within a picture. Here the materials were more abundant. For my purpose I have used chiefly his own writings, the "Cahier Rouge," the "Journal Intime," the autobiographical portions of "Adolphe," and letters. I have also used documents published by M. Rudler in his "Jeunesse de Benjamin Constant," a book which sifts his early years with scientific exactness.

The remarkable letter from Boswell to Zélide, of which portions appear in Chapter II, is in the library of Neuchâtel. As it is of great length I have quoted only the more personally relevant passages, especially as the entire text will, I hear, be included in Mr. C. B. Tinker's now impending collection of Boswell's Letters. I owe to his "Young Boswell" the reference to Rousseau in the same chapter.

My warm thanks are due to Mme. P. Godet and M. Marcel Godet for the kindness of their welcome, and for allowing me to use two silhouettes in their possession. I am indebted to M. E. Chenevière for assistance and introductions; to the Director of the Museum at Geneva for leave to reproduce La Tour's pastel; to the Director of the Museum at Neuchâtel for similar permission in regard to Houdon's bust; and more particularly to the library authorities at both these places for facilitating my examination of the MS. letters in their keeping.

VILLA MEDICI,

FLORENCE.   G.S.

October 23, 1924.

Scott's obsession with Zélide resulted from idle moments he and his wife, Lady Sybil, spent in Lausanne just after the First World War. They had come to Switzerland after Scott had suffered a nervous breakdown to visit the psychologist Dr. Roger Vittoz, whose world-renowned work on "brain control" attracted a privileged clientele, including Lady Ottoline Morrell. One rainy morning, after a session with the doctor, Scott discovered in a bookstore Philippe Godet's scholarly two-volume biography of Madame de Charrière, which had appeared in 1906. Scott and his wife spent many hours poring over the book's account of the eighteenth-century novelist's life.

As Scott wrote to a friend during those first few days of his research, "I am deep in a most fascinating book which has served as a distraction. It is called 'Madame de Charrière et ses Amis'—one of the best memoirs I have ever read & quite one of the most charming personalities. . . . The people it describes live as vitally as one's own acquaintances. But I think it contributed something to my despondency: Her life begins so vitally & brilliantly in her letters. You follow step by step the tragic dégringolade, or rather the increasing sense of isolation & of à quoi bon.

223

When I got to her death I felt as if I was being nailed into my own coffin. I have never, I think, felt such a vivid sense of being in another person's life except sometimes in reading Tolstoi. . . . My mind is full of her & of that period, & I am planning a book or a set of essays rather, per sfogarmi [to unburden myself], which I think might work out into something good." Scott was intrigued enough by Zélide's life for it to occupy much of his intellectual life over the next five years. The accidental discovery soon turned into a passion and helped to purge him from the despair that had brought him to Switzerland in the first place. At the end of his research, he wrote, "It is curious how intimately one gets to know the people one writes about. Mme. de Charrière is as real to me as almost anyone in actual life." The biographical, as is often the case, had become the autobiographical.

Geoffrey Scott was born in Hampstead in 1884, the son of a prosperous flooring manufacturer and his devout Unitarian wife. After time at Rugby, Scott matriculated at New College, Oxford, where his career was highlighted by the Newdigate Prize for poetry in 1906 and the Chancellor's Essay in 1908, devoted to a study of English architecture. He had pursued a course of study including Greek and Roman literature and philosophy, under the tutelage of Gilbert Murray, the preeminent classicist of his time.

His fully documented life began in 1906 when he and John Maynard Keynes, then a recent graduate of

King's College, Cambridge, arrived at Bernard and Mary Berenson's Villa I Tatti. Mary's sister, Bertrand Russell's wife, had proposed the two young men as guests to escort Mary and her daughters, the future sisters-in-law of Virginia Woolf and Lytton Strachey, on a motoring trip through Tuscany. By the end of the trip, a few weeks later, Scott had become Mary's protégé and would remain so until his marriage to the rich and seductive Lady Sybil Cutting, twelve years later.

During these years in Florence, Scott joined in architectural partnership with another young English friend of the Berensons, Cecil Pinsent. Their collaboration would result in renovations to the Villa I Tatti, including its much admired gardens, and the design of the Villa Le Balze for the American philosopher Charles Augustus Strong, John D. Rockefeller's son-in-law. During the same period, Scott's study of aesthetics resulted in *The Architecture of Humanism*, which had the misfortune of appearing a few days before the outbreak of the First World War. Contemporary reviewers made the book a succès d'estime and many architects came to consider Scott one of the most important architectural aestheticians of the century.

His marriage to Lady Sybil in 1918 precipitated a rupture with Mary Berenson and eventually led to her breakdown as well as his own. Scott, in his letters to friends, often compared his relationship with

Mary Berenson to Benjamin Constant's with Zélide and found this section of the book "embarrassing" to write. While a personal challenge to finish, the book firmly established his name as one of the period's great stylists and, at the same time, allowed him to venture forth into the world with a new sense of self-confidence.

His short-lived romance with Vita Sackville-West in 1923 and 1924 brought his marriage to an inevitable divorce, but the affair stimulated him to live up to his lover's growing literary reputation and her productivity spurred him to his most active period as a writer. Within two years, he published the second edition of *The Architecture of Humanism*, and a collection of poems, illustrated by Albert Rutherston, and at last finished *The Portrait of Zélide* for which he won the James Tait Black Memorial Prize.

The biography's great success led to a meeting with Colonel Ralph Isham in 1927 and to an offer to become the editor of the Boswell papers, which Isham had just begun to buy from the great eighteenth-century writer's descendants. Scott soon went to New York and for almost two years devoted his entire life to editing these papers. The result, the first six volumes of *The Private Papers of James Boswell from Malahide Castle*, was the beginning of a flood of Boswell texts which continues to this day and has become the most important English literary project of this century. Scott, however, died in New York in

1929, just after the appearance of the first volumes and the establishment of his reputation as a preeminent Boswell scholar.

Like Madame de Charrière, Geoffrey Scott is today hardly a household name. Very much a product of the elite English educational system, viewed by some as a reactionary in his aesthetic views, he is of little interest today to most scholars. But Scott remains to those who know his work an extremely compelling figure. A polymath, he felt comfortable among architects, humanists, poets, painters, socialites, and aristocrats. He was a man of extraordinary wit and charm, a stunning conversationalist who counted as close friends many of his most illustrious contemporaries, including Edith Wharton, John Maynard Keynes, the Berensons, the Duke of Wellington, and the Princess Thurn und Taxis. But Scott was above all a gifted writer, as *The Architecture of Humanism*, his prefaces to the Boswell papers, his unpublished correspondence, and especially *The Portrait of Zélide* demonstrate.

Richard Dunn